D1481034

The
COP
and the
KID

The COP and the KID

by WILLIAM FOX
with Noel Hynd

CONGDON & WEED, INC.
New York

Copyright © 1983 by William Fox and Gargoyle Productions, Inc.

Library of Congress Cataloging in Publication Data

Fox, William (William P.)
   The cop and the kid.

   1. Fox, William (William P.) 2. Police—New York (N.Y.)—Biogra-
phy. 3. Police services for juveniles—New York (N.Y.)—Case studies.
4. Youth—New York (N.Y.)—Suicidal behavior—Case studies. 5. Suicide
—New York (N.Y.)—Prevention—Case studies. 6. Rehabilitation of de-
linquents—New York (N.Y.)—Case studies. I. Hynd, Noel. II. Title.
HV8148.N5F69   1983   363.2′092′4   [B]   83-10098
ISBN 0-86553-086-6
ISBN 0-312-92101-2 (St. Martin's Press)

Published by Congdon & Weed, Inc.
298 Fifth Avenue, New York, N.Y. 10001
Distributed by St. Martin's Press
175 Fifth Avenue, New York, N.Y. 10010
Published simultaneously in Canada by Methuen Publications
2330 Midland Avenue, Agincourt, Ontario M1S 1P7

The events in this book are true. A few names, however, have been changed
to protect the privacy of certain individuals.

For
James and Lillian Fox
and
Eleanor Kunigonis
with
love and appreciation

The
COP
and the
KID

One

I am on my hands and knees in a Brooklyn tenement, crawling through a room filled with smoke. Outside I can hear the voices, the sirens, the sounds of heavy engines, and the orders barked over megaphones. But none of them seems quite real to me. What is real is that I am coughing violently and cannot get enough air. And I am clutching a child—a boy maybe six or seven months old—as I crawl through the smoke toward what I hope and pray is a window.

I am almost there, the window materializing through the blackness, when the floor beneath me begins to buckle. I see the sweating, sooty face of a fireman outside. But I cannot hear; suddenly everything is silent. With a final agonizing effort I rise to my knees and half pass, half throw the small boy to the fireman.

He reaches forward as far as he can. The flames dance around his gloves. Then he clutches the boy, pulling the child to safety, while underneath me the floor explodes and I fall screaming into the inferno below.

Then I wake, bolting upright in my bed, the scream still in my throat.

It takes me a moment to realize I have had my nightmare again. It keeps happening night after night. But I am safe in bed. Terrified, but safe.

I am covered with perspiration—the sweat of fear that I know so well. I glance at the clock beside my bed. It is 4:24 A.M. My pulse is racing and my mouth is parched. I get up from bed and go downstairs to the kitchen. I take a soda from the refrigerator and sit down at the kitchen table. The only sound is the ticking of the kitchen clock. But I am not yet ready to return to bed.

This nightmare recurs and recurs. I don't know how many times I've had it. It always ends the same way: the smoke, the fear, the scream in my throat, and the plunge into the fire. It keeps coming back because the first time it was not a dream. It actually happened.

That was a couple of years ago, in January 1980. I had been off duty at the time but heard a call for a nearby fire. I arrived to find a three-story building ablaze. Smoke was pouring from all the windows and ladders led up to some of them. The firemen were working with the hose when I turned and saw a woman shrieking and pointing at a second-story window. Her baby was upstairs.

What I did was not something I thought about. I acted because I knew I had to. Somehow I found the infant, but I had taken in so much smoke myself that I was dizzy and lost direction.

Seeing a glimmer of light, I ran toward it—and crashed into a plate-glass mirror. Stunned, I was just able to reason that the glimmer must have come from a window directly behind me. As I turned toward it, I passed out from smoke inhalation and a collapsed lung. The floor, however, did not actually give way until ninety seconds *after* two firemen had pulled me from the building.

In my mind, the fire is still burning. Something about it remains unsettled. Perhaps what I am dreaming about is the next fire. Would I go in again? I know the answer.

I recall the IV tubes, the tracheotomy, the priest giving me the last rites. I also remember a fellow police officer coming to see me a few days later. "Jeez," he said in hushed tones, waving his hand in a dismissing motion, "what'd you go in there for? They were just a bunch of spics. You coulda died."

"You wouldn't have gone in?"

"For another cop, yeah. For a member of my family, yeah."

The mother of the child I saved came to the hospital to thank me. She brought her son, a little olive-skinned boy who gave me a big smile and wrapped his tiny hand around my thumb.

I finish the can of soda, crumple it, ant toss it into the kitchen wastebasket. I go back upstairs and to sleep. In the hour that remains before my alarm clock wakes me, I do not dream again.

You need to know only a few things about me. My name is Bill Fox and I was born in Brooklyn, New York, thirty-seven years ago. My father is dead. My mother and I share the two-story house on Van Duzer Street in Staten Island where I was raised. My sister and two brothers have homes and families of their own. Though I've twice been engaged to be married, I am still a bachelor. So I have never bothered to move out. Many years ago, my ancestors came to America

11

from County Killkenny, Ireland. I have never been to County Killkenny, but someday I'd love to visit.

I am probably a lot like you. I consider myself an average guy trying to do an honest day's work and live my life with a certain set of ethics and principles. Where possible, I try to help people.

My job is the only thing that separates me from others. Since 1973, I have been one of the two hundred men assigned to the Emergency Services Squad, under the command of Inspector Daniel St. John. I am assigned to Truck Number One at 230 East Twenty-first Street in Manhattan, just next to the busy Thirteenth Precinct and through the block from the Policy Academy. The One Truck, as we call it, is a twenty-two-foot long, thirteen-ton mechanized Goliath—a cross between a moving van and a truck. Decked out in functional blue and white NYPD colors, it bears the Police Department insignia on both sides, and has the somewhat cryptic words INTERNATIONAL/DIESEL/FLEETSTAR in small metal block letters across its front grill. The One Truck sits in its garage and growls when it is not in use. There are men assigned to it at all times and it is always ready.

The One Truck and the six smaller R.E.P. vans (Radio Emergency Patrol) that cruise the borough and act as satellites for the One Truck are equipped for any sort of urban Armageddon. We carry—and every man in our unit is an expert in the use of—acetylene torches, grappling hooks, emergency power generators, resuscitators, floodlights, Geiger counters, pipe and wire cutters, infrared viewers, compressed oxygen, wood chocks, a horse belt, animal lassos, smoke and blast grenades, tear gas guns, life nets, bomb blankets, tow chains, sewer plates, Kelly bars, Hurst tools, Halligan tools, air packs, anti-sniper carbines, .30-30s, 9-mm submachine guns, helmets, bullet-proof vests, flak jackets, rescue saws, wool blankets, screw-jacks, riot shields, and body bags.

A slogan in our Emergency Handbook reads: *When a civilian needs help, he calls a cop. When a cop needs help, he calls Emergency Services.* We are called into situations that have escaped the control of the local precincts. So whether it's a raccoon in an attic or the end of the world, we're ready.

Two

EARLY one morning in April I am at my locker, changing from civilian clothes into my uniform.

Gary Gorman, my best friend and usual partner, is a few lockers away putting on his bullet-proof vest, a hot, heavy tunic-style garment. "Don't forget the vest, Billy," he says to me.

"Already got it," I answer, pulling aside a button of my shirt to show him.

Down the row of lockers, two other good friends are also changing. Paul Redecha and Al Sheppard. Often the four of us work together or, if one of us is sick or on vacation, we interchange partners. We have worked as each other's back-ups several times, too. Somehow things seem to happen to us. In our unit we are nicknamed the Gang of Four, not always appreciatively.

Tom McCarthy saunters by, eyeing the vests, particularly

14

Gary's. McCarthy has been one of the top Emergency men in the city for the past fifteen years. But recently nothing has been right.

He stops and looks at us, a cigarette burning between the yellowed fingers of his right hand. McCarthy is on his way off duty. He has removed his shield and his black clip-on tie.

"What are you guys messing with those things for?" he asked derisively. McCarthy, like some of the older cops, has a fixation about the vests.

"Knock it off, Tommy," Gary says.

"Sheppard doesn't wear a vest," McCarthy continues, looking for an ally. "What's the matter with the rest of you?"

"Sheppard thinks he's Superman," I answer. "He doesn't think he bleeds."

"He spent too much time in Vietnam," Redecha says, trying to get rid of McCarthy. "Didn't get hit there so he doesn't think he can get whacked out here."

"That's got nothing to do with it," Sheppard says, lighting a cigarette. "The vest is hot. Uncomfortable. I don't like it." Shep shrugs. "In this outfit I usually got time to put a flak jacket on if I need it, anyway."

"'Usually?'" I asked Sheppard. Shep rolls his eyes in response.

"Yeah, but that's what I mean," McCarthy persists. "I mean, Emergency isn't an arrest-oriented squad like Tactical Patrol was or like Senior Citizens' Anti-crime. Most emergency work now is fishing floaters out of the Hudson or breaking into locked cars. And when you go on a sniper job or have a barricade you can put on the flak suits. So I don't understand these vests."

"When you were our age, Tommy," I tell him, "they didn't have the firepower that's out there now."

"Aaah, bullshit!" he says. "What good are the vests? When they shoot at you these days, they aim for your brains or your jock strap."

Gary and I continue dressing. Neither of us says anything.

"Plus, they got ammunition on the street today that'll chop right through those cheap things. You might as well go out there bare-assed, boys."

"I'll bet he was wearing a vest himself the night President Garfield was shot," I mumble to Gary, who grins. What McCarthy says about the vests is only a cloak for the petty feuding that goes on within the squad.

The real issue is between the older guys who think some of us take the job too seriously and the younger guys who think the oldtimers don't take the job seriously enough.

McCarthy is right about one thing, though. There is ammunition out there now, in the hands of the wrong people, that can pierce any vest made. It is manufactured right here in the United States, and it is used primarily to wound or kill police officers. There is a bill in Congress that would outlaw its sale to anyone outside of the police department. Both the manufacturers and the National Rifle Assocation plan to fight the bill, claiming that it's unfair to deprive sportsmen of this new product. I don't know how some people sleep at night.

The Gray Table is our social club, our life raft, and our psychiatric couch, where the men on the squad kick around the latest rumor before work or rake over a fellow officer after. It's the place we discuss the job or a guy who isn't pulling his weight. Actually it's several tables, shoved together, battered, scratched, and all the same depressing battleship gray.

This morning we have a television crew in search of a story. Besides the cameraman and a soundman there is a third fellow who looks around the room, smiling tentatively. I know what he is doing. He is trying to decide which two-man team his crew would follow. The next twelve minutes before our shift begins is story time.

Georgie Toth tells about the day a woman reported a lion sitting on the ledge of her apartment building. To begin with, the precinct that took the call thought the woman was a crank. After she'd called back a second and then a third time, four Emergency men found themselves in a small garden behind a loft building in Soho. Across a skimpy wooden fence was one fully grown lion, his mane rippling in the breeze.

Toth and his partner, Mike McCrory, recalled that the circus was in town, featuring a man who billed himself as the world's greatest lion tamer. One of the R.E.P.'s shot over to Madison Square Garden while two Emergency men kept a wary eye on the cat. The lion, meanwhile, was amusing himself by taking bites out of an old rubber tire and tearing apart a plaster mannequin.

At the Garden the Emergency men found the lion tamer and told him what they had.

"Does the cat have his back teeth?" the lion tamer asked.

"We haven't exactly gotten close enough to see."

"Has he been declawed?"

"Doesn't look that way."

"Has he been tranquilized?"

"No, sir."

"Then I'm not going near him and you shouldn't either," said the world's greatest lion tamer.

Six Emergency cops teamed up to lasso the animal, edged it into a portable cage, and whisked it up to the Central Park Zoo. There, the animal refused to leave the cage.

Finally an Emergency man named Jess Upshaw got angry

enough to give the cat a gentle kick in the rear. Whereupon, with a thunderous roar, the cat burst forth and bolted into a waiting cage, while some brave soul ran forward to slam the door shut.

"Want to know the best part?" Toth asks the camera crew. "The guy who was keeping the lion said it wasn't his. He said he was only watching it for a friend."

Now Paul Redecha and Al Sheppard tell about being assigned to guard the Shah of Iran when he was being treated for cancer at New York Hospital. They recount warnings by the Shah's men of possible helicopter attacks by an anti-Shah force from Queens, and the parade of celebrities that came through—including Barbara Walters, Henry Kissinger, and Frank Sinatra.

"Sinatra wasn't a bad guy at all," Sheppard says. "Always said hello when he went by. Kissinger was the funniest. We were in plainclothes and he nearly jumped out of his skin when he saw each of us had automatic rifles sitting next to our chairs."

"How about Barbara Walters?" one of the film crew asks.

Sheppard grins. "That was funny, too. She brought this beautiful big pie for the Shah and gave it to his security people. They bowed and thanked her. Then as soon as she was out of sight they threw it in the garbage. Afraid someone had laced it with poison." Sheppard shrugs and snuffs out a cigarette. "What a waste, right?"

The mood around the Gray Table is light this morning, the feuding all but invisible. The camera crew isn't aware that certain cops never speak directly to certain other cops. And as the television crew selects a team to follow, and I wish them luck, I know that there are certain stories, such as those about Stephen Gilroy or Patrick O'Connor, that will not be told on occasions like this.

18

Gilroy was an Emergency cop assigned to Brooklyn. In August 1978 he responded to the report of an armed robbery at a Brooklyn sporting goods store. The gunmen were cornered inside, and for several hours they sniped at the Emergency teams in flak jackets who ringed the store. During a lull in the shooting, Gilroy raised his head to see what was happening. A rifle bullet struck him between the eyes and killed him instantly.

Pat O'Connor's was an entirely different situation. Thanksgiving eve, back in 1971, Pat and his partner were driving an R.E.P. on the Brooklyn-Queens Expressway. Near Fifty-eighth Street they stopped to help a woman motorist who was trying to change a flat tire. Pat was hit by a drunken driver in a truck.

Pat worked out of our house on Twenty-first Street. There is a bronze plaque for him there. It bears his likeness, in uniform and laughing—which is the way his comrades remember him—with the words:

> In Memoriam
> Ptl. Patrick O'Connor
> Killed in the line of duty
> November 24, 1971
> Greater love has no man
> than he who lays down his life
> for his friends.

The plaque is the first thing we see coming up the steps to report to work and the last thing we see when we leave—a reminder of what every precinct and fire house in the city must live with.

Often, after a cop is killed in the line of duty, it is easier to remember what happened to him than to remember his name. You conceptualize the man's death by what happened, how he got into the position of vulnerability that led to his death, and what the last seconds must have been like. Maybe this is because you know you could have been there and that you might have dropped your guard in the same manner. You try to make a mental note not to.

Frank Cecil Sledge is a name I will always remember. He died one night while I was in the hospital recovering from the collapsed lung.

I was in the Sixty-eighth Precinct at the time, and Sledge was in the Sixty-ninth—which for some reason is not right next door but all the way across Brooklyn, encompassing Flatlands and Canarsie. On the night of January 28, 1980, while he was on patrol, Frank stopped a car at Flatlands Avenue and East Seventy-eighth Street. The occupant, a young man with wild dark hair and a devilish-looking goatee, was known in the neighborhood as Crazy Sal. He liked to strut around with his shirt off, displaying the winged skull he had tattooed on his chest. The two were old antagonists, and on the night Officer Sledge stopped the car, Crazy Sal was on parole from a prison for robbing a woman at knifepoint.

Words were exchanged as the patrolman approached the car. Shots were fired. A moment later, the car backed up, trapping Officer Sledge's body in its undercarriage, and roared off along Flatlands Avenue at sixty miles an hour, leaving a trail of blood behind. Sal was arrested two days later, a block or two away from the spot where Officer Sledge died. His plea was that he had run over the officer in self-defense. A year later, a jury would see things differently. This time, Crazy Sal would be convicted of second-degree murder and sentenced to twenty-five years in prison.

But Frank Sledge was dead, and there was something about the way he died that every officer would remember.

Over and over, we replayed the death of Frank Sledge in our minds and in the locker room.

"The guy in the car got off the first shot," somebody said. "Frank couldn't see the punk's hands."

"They got phosphorus lights along Flatlands," a cop who used to work the Six-nine pointed out.

"Yeah," I said, "but the lights glare. You can see the street but you can't see inside a car."

"Do you believe the fucker is claiming that Frank opened fire on him first?" an officer named O'Brien said bitterly.

"I believe anything," said another cop.

How had Frank Sledge let someone like Crazy Sal get off the first shot at him? What was the mistake he had made? We wanted to know, because none of us ever wanted to die under a speeding auto with a bullet in the chest.

I had reason to remember this conversation a couple of months later.

It was during the transit strike that began on the first of April. The strike put more people on the streets and gave most officers in the five boroughs twelve-hour shifts for an indefinite period.

A twelve-hour shift is rugged enough. But the one that ended in the early hours of April 6 proved a nightmare for me.

My partner, Mike Richardson, and I had been the back-up team on a shooting. We had investigated a mugging and two burglaries. At 4 A.M. we'd been the first car on the scene at a homicide on Twelfth Avenue in Brooklyn. We were already tired when the call to any available unit came over the radio.

"WE GOT A TEN THIRTY IN BAY RIDGE. INVESTIGATE SUSPICIOUS CAR, WHITE BUICK NEW YORK LICENSE ONE FOUR SEVEN ADAM BOY EDWARD."

Mike, a rookie, was driving. A ten thirty was a burglary in

progress. As Central blurted the address of a liquor store on Fourth Avenue, I said to him, "Let's take a look. Go down Fifth Avenue."

We used no lights or sirens, in the hope of converging quietly with any other cars that might be responding.

I picked up the radio to let headquarters know we were responding as we cut across Eighty-sixth Street through a red light and turned southward onto Fifth Avenue. I noted on my log sheet that the time had been 6:23 when we picked up the call.

"Take a look," Mike said a minute later, as he motioned to a long white car a block and a half ahead of us. From that distance I could see the car was maybe a seventy or seventy-one, with rusted fenders. I squinted. "Two males," I said. Again we ran a light, and I could feel my pulse quicken. In the way it moved down the street this car looked dirty and acted dirty.

We got to within half a block, and I could see the license plates. "That's them," I said to Mike.

I picked up the radio to report: "SIX EIGHT DAVID TO CENTRAL. WE HAVE THE WHITE BUICK. WE'RE STOPPING IT. REQUEST BACK-UP."

I hit the lights and the siren as our patrol car bolted forward. We were directly behind the Buick now. It speeded up briefly, then slowed as it went through a red light at Ninetieth Street and rolled to a halt at Ninety-second Street.

We got out and approached the car, Mike taking the driver's side and I the passenger's.

"Be careful," I said to the rookie.

I stood a few feet from the rear door with my right hand near my gun. Mike went to the driver's window.

I checked the license plate and description of the vehicle

again. This was the suspicious car. I scanned the backseat for stolen goods or burglary tools but I saw nothing, meaning everything was probably in the trunk or already ditched.

Then I kept my eyes on the two white males in the front seat. They were in their late teens or early twenties, shaggy-haired and unshaven.

"License and registration," Mike said, acting cautiously.

"Sure thing, officer," the driver said. "Did I do something wrong?"

He handed Mike two pieces of paper from the top of the dashboard. There seemed something wrong in the way he handed them over, so I left my position, moving forward slightly to see better.

Where the hell are our back-ups? I wondered, cursing the transit department and the strike that was causing us to be overworked and undermanned. Just then I saw the driver's hand move slowly down his leg. The light was bad. But as I leaned forward, I saw the hand go for the ankle—and that he had a pistol there.

"Mike!" I yelled. "He's got a weapon!" I tried to spring back but now everything was happening at once—the passenger lunging halfway out the window to grab my left arm, Mike hitting the ground, and then bolting away from the car.

I heard the tires squeal and felt an excrutiating pain in my shoulder as the passenger pulled my arm into the car and cranked up the window until it was like a vise and would go no farther.

Trapped against the side of the car as it began to move, trying desperately to remain upright and failing, I thought, *Frank Sledge! This was how they killed Frank Sledge. Dragged him through Brooklyn. Torn apart under a speeding car.*

The certainty of death flashed through my mind as I lost

balance, feeling the warmth and wetness of my own blood spurting as the hipbone dragged along the ground.

Somehow, with my free hand, I managed to extract my pistol from the mangled shreds of its holster. Drawing on every bit of strength I had left I raised it and pointed it toward the car door—only to be given pause by one final thought: if I shot the driver and killed him, the car would go rushing on until it crashed. Pinned there beside the window, I could burn to death. On the other hand, if I aimed for his foot, got his foot off the accelerator—

I aimed low and began to fire.

The car shuddered, fishtailed, and swerved, brushing against a series of parked cars as it careened, nearly turned over on me, and then skidded to a halt.

By now I was losing consciousness. I was distantly aware of sirens, the pain that was everywhere, a commotion around me while the man in the car fled on foot. And of blue uniforms.

Someone placed a blanket on me. I could not move my legs.

Paralyzed, I thought. Better to die.

For an instant everything was very bright. Then I lost consciousness.

Several hours later, I recognized the blurry, dull feeling that goes with pain-killing drugs.

My brother Jimmy was looking down at me.

"You done it again, kid," he said.

He told me I was in Lutheran General Hospital in Brooklyn. That had been the hospital closest to the scene. A patrol car had rushed me there seconds after I'd passed out.

"You got some important visitors," Jimmy said. My eyes would not quite focus, but I could see two men standing there. One of them was balding with prominent features. The other was shorter, stockier, and obviously Irish. He asked, "How you feeling, officer?"

"Not so bad," I mumbled, my voice dragging. "Lucky to be here, I guess."

"We arrested the two suspects," he said. "We got the guys who put you in here."

"Oh," I said, trying to recall the incident, remembering the blanket being put over me.

"Good," I added blankly.

There seemed to be a silence in the room and I thought, *My legs!* Then I found that though everything hurt, I could still move.

"The Police Department has a car assigned to your mother," the shorter man was saying. "She can use it to come and go from the hospital and to get around. We'll take care of things while you're here." As I squinted at him, the recognition flashed: John J. McGuire, the Police Commissioner.

"The doctors tell me you've got a chipped hipbone," the other man was saying, "some internal bleeding, bruises, and flesh wounds."

"That's all?" I asked, trying to smile.

I studied the face.

"Officer," he went on, "I just want you to know that you'll have the best treatment in the city. If my office can do anything for you and your family, I've asked your brothers to let us know."

I blinked twice, and though I now had a thundering headache, I extended my hand.

"Thank you, Mr. Mayor," I said.

Two things saved my life: the bullet-proof vest, which prevented my ribs from splintering, and the bullet I had fired.

It passed just above the accelerator, crashed through the floor panels, and entered the engine block. There it ricocheted. It struck the oil pan, blowing a massive hole through which the oil poured from the engine and onto the street. With no lubrication left, the pistons jammed, the car stalled, and I survived.

I would be in the hospital, flat on my back, for several weeks. During that time I had a lot to think about.

Three

MICHAEL

MICHAEL'S earliest recollections were of his father; never his mother. But he truly knew his grandparents.

His father was around when Michael was small. Michael could recall that much. Yet his father would go off for a few days here and there. And he always seemed to have a different job.

Grandma—his father's mother—would make chicken twice a week for Michael because that was his favorite meal. Chicken and dumplings with iced tea. Ft. Worth, Texas, was their home. And when the season was right, Michael and his grandpa would go outside to a big old pecan tree—the one they said had been there longer than Texas had been a state—and pick big fat pecans. Then they'd crack them, shell them, pick out the meat, and bring them to the table. Grandpa was good at it and showed Michael how to shell pecans.

There were neighbors and a lot of lazy Sunday afternoons. And there was school, of course, but Michael had friends and was doing well.

No one ever mentioned Michael's mother. Grandma and Grandpa's expression would only darken when her name came up, and his father had once cursed violently and said she was no good.

The Vietnam War was going on at the time and Michael's dad was over there for two years. Grandma was worried about him even though she said that he wasn't always the best son she could have hoped for. Then the war ended and Michael's father came home. He seemed moodier now.

Michael turned eight years old in March 1972 and a few days later Grandma was in tears. "Don't go upstairs, Michael," someone said softly.

Michael knew before anyone sat him down and told him. God had taken Grandpa during the night. He'd passed away peacefully in his sleep; that much was a blessing.

Michael's dad barely knew how to handle it. But the worst part was Grandma. She was inconsolable and cried and cried. A month later, she died too. The doctors said she died of a broken heart. No will to live.

Mike's world started to crumble. There was no more chicken and no more dumplings. And no more climbing in the pecan tree. His father didn't seem very interested in him.

Dad would be gone all weekend sometimes and would forget to stock the refrigerator. Michael wasn't sure where his father was until he came home Sunday evening tired and looking like he'd drunk too much. And he was always talking on the phone to women and then disappearing again.

Once when his father returned from a lost weekend, he found Michael crying under a bridge. Dragging him home, he beat him. Soon thereafter a problem developed. Michael would wake up in the middle of the night and his bed would be soaking wet. Dad beat him for that too.

More and more Michael wished he had a mother. Other boys had moms. Even if their fathers thrashed them or drank or messed with women, all the other guys had a Mom to turn to. So one day Michael asked his father about his own Mom.

"You want to know, don't you?" he drawled. "You want to know what kind of woman she is, huh?"

"Yes, sir," Michael said.

"You know why you're with me, Michael?" his dad continued. "Your Ma didn't want you. Didn't love you at all. Wanted to get rid of you. That's why you got taken away from her and given to me."

One evening a few weeks later, the boy's father spread out on the kitchen table a map of the southern United States. Ft. Worth, which seemed so big, was smaller than a dime on the map.

"When things don't go well for you in one place," said Michael's father, who was currently unemployed, "you pick up and go somewhere else. Ain't nothing stopping you."

Father and son stared at the map. Then Michael's dad pointed to Ft. Worth. "This is where we are," he said. Then he ran his finger upward to the right. "And this is where we're going." The finger stopped at Memphis, Tennessee.

Two mornings later, father and son packed all their belongings into a yellow 1966 Pontiac GTO. And off they went.

In Memphis they checked into a motel and the father found work. He was running a booth at the Memphis in May Carnival. Michael was supposed to stay in the motel room during the day, which he did mostly, especially since there was a color television. But he was restless.

Sometimes at night it was difficult to sleep. Michael's dad would come home late and often with a woman. They stayed in the room and the boy was put out in the hall.

There was a nice old cleaning lady who came by every morning and Michael liked to talk to her. Her name was Hilda. But she couldn't stay and talk long because she had to do all the rooms by ten each day.

Michael wanted to go to the carnival, too, and he kept asking his father to take him. Finally his dad agreed. They drove there one morning and his father stepped out of the GTO.

"You wait here for a minute," he said. "I'll get a pass for you."

Michael sat in the car and waited. The minute turned into hours. Daylight turned into evening. Evening became night.

Michael started to cry. He left the car and went to the front gate of the carnival. "Can I get in without a ticket?" he asked a security guard. He had no money.

The guard smiled and shook his head. "Nope," he said. "Got to buy a ticket."

The boy said his father was inside and he'd been waiting in the car all day.

The guard's expression changed. Another guard appeared and they put the boy in their car and drove him all over the Memphis in May Carnival grounds until he spotted his dad.

Michael smiled and waved.

His father was furious. "You get back in the car!" he shouted. "I'll deal with you later!"

Michael knew what that meant and dreaded the moment they'd drive back to the motel. He prayed there would be a woman to distract his father. But there wasn't.

The next morning when Hilda opened the door she found Michael semi-conscious and covered with scars and bruises. She called the motel manager and the motel manager called the Memphis police.

Michael was hospitalized. He did not see his father for several weeks, but heard that he had been arrested. Then there was a court hearing to which Michael was taken by a social worker.

"Don't be afraid," she told him. "All this will be for the best."

Michael answered a few questions for the court. His father hardly looked at him, gazing straight ahead without expression.

The court made Michael Lynn Buchanan a ward of the State of Tennessee. His father was held liable for his support. Michael's dad was also given two years to straighten out his life and come back to claim his son. Meanwhile, the state would look after Michael. The court adjourned.

Michael's dad bolted to his feet to leave. Michael started to cry and turned toward the judge.

"I want to live with my father! I want to live with my father!" he implored. But the judge only gazed at him sadly and shook his head. The court's decision had been rendered and was final. The social worker took Michael by the hand and consoled him as best she could.

Four

I come from a religious family. All four of us kids—Eileen, Jimmy, Roddy, and I—went to St. Patrick's School in the Bay Ridge Section of Brooklyn, where I lived until I was fifteen. While I was in the sixth grade there, I told my parents that I wanted to be a priest.

They were surprised, as I guess most parents would be—particularly if this announcement came from a boy of twelve. My father was a conductor for the New York City Transit Authority—one of those guys who peer out of a car in the middle of the train, making sure the doors close properly and everyone is safely aboard. My older brother Jimmy had decided by then that he wanted to become a policeman—as both he and Roddy eventually did. But at St. Patrick's School, I had developed a special admiration for a priest whose name was Father Lynch.

One night there had been a terrible fire in the neighborhood, within sight of St. Patrick's, in which three out of a family of five had perished. One of the victims had been a classmate of mine.

Father Lynch was on the scene along with the firemen, giving what comfort he could to the two shattered survivors. The next morning he visited our classroom and spoke softly of the tragedy, reminding us that death is a part of life. I already knew how much Father Lynch meant to the people of the neighborhood. But I think that incident made me resolve to be like him.

Then there was the night a few years later when my brothers and sister and I were awakened by a commotion downstairs. The four of us quickly gathered at the landing. The clock showed a few minutes after eleven—far too early for my father to be home from his night shift. But there he was, sitting next to Mother, his arm around her but his face ashen. Two strapping New York City policemen were with them.

"Hey," one called out good-naturedly when they noticed us. "Back to bed. Everything's going to be all right."

Then I saw what they must have been trying to keep from us—my father's blue Transit Authority shirt, slashed and soaked with blood. He'd been attacked on the subway by a rampaging youth gang. Some transit cops had broken up the assault and the attackers had fled, after stabbing him nine or ten times in the chest, arms, and back. The two policemen had brought him home from the emergency room at Bellevue, where it had taken fifty-eight stitches to close the wounds. Their green-and-white patrol car was sitting in front of our house, its parking lights on.

Watching the two men leave, I felt a rush of gratitude for the calm and dedication they had brought to the situation. In a certain tough, street-wise way, they reminded me of Father Lynch.

My father went back to work as soon as his wounds had healed. But the incident aged him, and I don't think my mother ever slept well again before he got home from a night's work.

Not long afterward, he applied for a job with the New York State Thruway and was accepted. I was overjoyed. We had spent a number of summer vacations near the town of Newburgh, where my sister and brothers and I would work on a local farm—picking vegetables, milking cows, and feeding chickens, watering the crops, and throwing rotten apples at each other. We all loved it up there. Now we would be living on a farm of our own, while my father worked on the Thruway. He drew on his pension with the Transit Authority to make a down payment, but that is not the sort of detail a kid worries about.

Things didn't turn out too well. My father was soon transferred farther upstate at a 20 percent cut in pay. My mother worked at a local inn, doing housekeeping jobs, to bring in a few extra dollars. That left my two brothers, my sister, and me to work the farm—six acres of apple trees, two acres each of pears and peaches. The day I took in my first dollar for a basket of apples, I felt as though the world belonged to me. But the economy that summer turned rotten as a peach in the sun. There weren't enough dollars coming in to meet the payments on the farm and make a profit. We stayed on through a discouraging fall and the bleakest winter I ever hope to spend. One sub-zero day the pump froze. And I could give you a hundred and fifty different recipes for meals based on the apples we couldn't sell. Such as apple stew or an apple omelette.

When at last we couldn't make the mortage payments, the

bank foreclosed, leaving us disillusioned though maybe a little tougher and a little wiser. My father went back to work for the Transit Authority, and we moved into a house on Staten Island.

In Staten Island, we lived on the borderline between two parishes, a circumstance that greatly enriched my life. I was more serious than ever about becoming a priest. And I got to know two men whom I greatly respected—Father McGinn at Immaculate Conception and Father Sheehan at St. Sylvester's. I began spending as much time as I could assisting both men in church and community projects.

One day I asked Father McGinn, a young-looking man in his late thirties, if I could meet with him at his rectory. I was on time for the interview and came straight to the point about wanting to be a priest.

A long and searching conversation followed. We spent most of the day in his office talking. Finally he said, "I'd like you to consider the Third Order of St. Francis. It's a teaching and educational order. I think you'd fit in well with them, Bill."

He told me about a Franciscan seminary in Staten Island. Over the next few months I began spending my weekends there. I felt at home. I liked the people, the tranquility, and the solid feeling of mission. I began to understand why the word "calling" is used and what it could mean. With each visit, I became more convinced than ever that this was what I wanted to do with my life.

After several months, Father McGinn gave me a letter recommending me to the Franciscan order. He told me that after an interview before a governing board of local priests, I'd be able to enter the Franciscan seminary any time I chose. I was elated.

*   *   *

But things were not easy at home. My father had withdrawn most of his pension from the Transit Authority to buy the farm we had lost. The money was gone. And the years of working underground had taken their toll.

He had advancing arthritis, a recurrent ulcer, and the doctors didn't like the sound of his heart. He had run out of sick days and had exhausted his medical insurance.

My brother Jimmy had become a police recruit, gotten married, and moved to a home of his own. I was now the oldest son in the house. I needed work, so I began learning the electrician's craft from a neighbor named Irv Christenson who was generous enough to teach me. I continued my high school classes at night. Eileen and Roddy went during the day.

In September 1963, when I was eighteen, my father went into the hospital for an operation on a duodenal ulcer. The operation was not supposed to be a serious one.

A few nights later, the telephone rang at 3 A.M. I can still remember that it sounded five times before my mother picked it up. No one calls with good news at three in the morning. At the age of fifty-one, my father was dead of cardiac arrest.

Not long thereafter, at the age of twenty, I found myself up on a scaffolding inside a movie theater, completing a wiring job. Suddenly I felt a pain my my chest. Soon it was so intense I couldn't breath.

There was little doubt in my mind that I was having a heart attack and that I too was dying.

What followed is no more than an unpleasant blur. I was taken to St. Vincent's Hospital in Staten Island, where the doctors concluded that my problem was appendicitis. And after my appendix had been removed, I began to feel better.

36

A few days later I left the hospital and before long I returned to work. For about a week everything was fine.

Then the same thing happened all over again, only this time the pain and shortness of breath were worse.

I was now treated for a duodenal ulcer. But there was no relief. The pain and the symptoms persisted. My skin became jaundiced and I was losing weight. The doctors decided I had hepatitis and for several weeks I was treated for this. But I could feel myself growing weaker, and when the pain flared up again it became apparent that no one knew what was wrong with me.

Friends and relatives I hadn't seen for years began coming to visit me. One day when my brother Jimmy was alone with me, I asked him, "What are the doctors telling these people?"

"They say you're real sick," was Jimmy's first answer. "They think seeing people may boost your morale."

"Level with me," I insisted.

He looked me firmly in the eye. "They think you're a goner."

The emotions that surged within me were so powerful that I had to look away from my brother. "They're wrong!" I snapped back at him. "I'm Irish! I don't go down for the count without a good long fight!"

"Yeah," he said. "I know. You'll lick it, Billy."

I clasped his hand again, but his strong hand holding my weak one only brought me back to reality.

Father McGinn and Father Sheehan both came to see me. They were reassuring. Spiritually, I could accept my fate. Physically, it was another matter. And now on top of this my health insurance had run out.

One day there was a knock at the door and a hospital administrator, a young man with wavy hair and glasses, came in. He introduced himself and told me that there was a very capable internal specialist from Chicago who would be in New York the following week. "He's had considerable success with cases like yours."

"What do you mean, cases like mine?" I asked.

"Cases that have eluded diagnosis."

Suddenly this *was* good news. "So he will come to see me?" I asked.

"Well, he can if..."

"If what?"

"He charges five hundred dollars for an initial visit and consultation," the administrator told me. He glanced down at some papers he held. "It says here that your insurance has run out."

The hospital's real concern was so clear that I felt a surge of energy and rage I hadn't experienced for weeks. "Jesus Christ!" I yelled at the guy, throwing off my sheets as my visitor wisely bolted toward the door.

I was dragging the IV line and the bottle of fluid suspended on the IV pole, and after two steps the adrenalin was gone.

I don't remember hitting the floor. And I never saw the specialist.

But now my family found a new doctor named Richard Stark, a true gentleman as well as a gifted physician. Seven months had passed since I'd first fallen ill on the scaffolding. I had lost sixty pounds. Dr. Stark started the entire examination procedure all over again and somehow succeeded where others had failed.

One Friday afternoon he was ready to talk with me. "I think I've located the problem," he began. "You have gall stones and a burst bladder." The stones, he explained, were causing the pain. And the burst gall bladder had given me both a blood infection and a related infection of the liver.

Though another round of surgery was needed, there was an added complication.

He showed me a very busy-looking chart.

"What's that all about?" I asked.

"This is your blood count," he said, pointing to a line and some numbers above a shaded area. "And this," he added as his finger dropped to the shaded area, "is where a normal blood count should be. Yours is dangerously elevated."

"Doc, I'm not in here be ause I'm healthy," I said, forcing a smile.

"Operating with your level this elevated risks a serious extra shock or trauma to your system," he said. "And your body just can't take much more."

He lowered the chart and held my gaze.

"You mean it could kill me?" I said.

He nodded.

"You *can't* operate but you *must* operate." I said. "That's it?"

"That's it," he said. Waiting too long, hoping for the levels to drop, could prove fatal. Operating with the levels still elevated could also prove fatal.

"And you're asking me to choose?" I asked.

"I'm asking you to understand," he said firmly.

A few hours later, Father Sheehan came in. "We're going to say a Mass for you on Sunday, Bill. Everyone's going to be there. Your friends. Your scout group." He tried to make me smile. "I'm glad we have a large church," he said, reaching to take my hand. Then he gave me the last rites.

That day I had plenty of time to begin to put things in perspective. How could I have once gotten so upset over the little things in life? A broken dinner plate. A parking ticket. A television that stopped working. What mattered was the way

I lived my life. Could I now look back and be happy? Could I honestly say that I had tried to do the right things most of the time? Had I made a better world for those around me?

In the late afternoon, I was given a dose of Demerol and drifted into an uneasy sleep that lasted into the next day.

That evening, Sunday, Dr. Stark appeared by my beside. This was not the hour he usually came.

"Welcome back," he said to me. He had a folder in his hands.

"Feeling any better?" he asked.

"Maybe some." Trying to drag myself out of the Demerol-induced sleep, I shook my head.

Dr. Stark was studying my chart. "What have you been doing here today?" he asked.

"Doing?" I said in disbelief. "I've been lying here on my back for the last twenty-four hours."

"Nobody gave you any medicines? Injections?"

"They drew some blood. I don't know when."

"That was this afternoon. I'm looking at the results." He indicated the folder.

It suddenly occurred to me that Dr. Stark had come to the hospital for a specific reason. "What's going on?" I asked. "What else is wrong?"

"Nothing's wrong. Something is right for a change."

The figures that had been dangerously elevated forty-eight hours earlier had plummeted that Sunday afternoon and were now at an acceptable level.

"I can't explain this," he said. "But the results are accurate. I even had a second series of tests done. I won't argue, but I've never seen anything like it."

All I could think of was Father Sheehan at St. Sylvester's that morning. I felt a bumpy sensation at the base of my scalp.

"They said a Mass for me today," I told Dr. Stark.

He shook his head in admiration and astonishment. "Somebody somewhere is keeping an eye on you, Fox. We can operate tomorrow. I think you might walk out of this hospital after all."

The operation took eight hours. The surgeons removed my gall bladder, three gall stones, and a piece of my liver. They also replaced a common duct with a link of plastic.

"Plastic?" I asked afterward. "Inside to stay?"

They kidded me, saying that it was like putting a new hose in an automobile's fuel line. And I was glad to be in a position to laugh.

My appetite returned, along with my ability to digest food. In a few weeks, I was up and a short time after that, I was home. My stay in the hospital had lasted thirteen months. I couldn't even remember my twenty-first birthday.

But I was alive. I had been spared. And I've little doubt as to what happened in the hospital. Only a person of faith could accept it, I suppose, but I will always feel that God took over.

One of the first visits I made out of the hospital was to Father Sheehan at St. Sylvester's.

"You know, Father," I said to him, "I figure there was a good reason why I was spared. I don't know what it is now. Maybe someday I will." Quickly, and a little nervously, I forged on. "The problem is, Father," I continued, "I'm no longer sure about becoming a priest. In some ways I want to more than ever. But I'm also fifteen thousand dollars in debt from this illness."

As always, he understood. "If the priesthood is your calling, it will wait for you," he assured me. "If not this year, next year. If not next year, in five years or ten. But you know," he continued, "there are other ways to serve God, your faith and mankind. And I'm certain that has occurred to you."

He was reading my mind, making it easier for me. "Yes, Father. It has."

"Tell me what you are thinking."

I drew a long breath. "My younger brother has become a policeman. My older brother has been one for four years. And my sister is married to one."

Father Sheehan began to smile.

"I'm surrounded by them, Father. I may have a thick, stubborn skull, but I'm beginning to get the message."

I went on talking about the possibility of police work. Father Sheehan held up his hand.

"Bill," he said, arching his thick eyebrows. "You don't have to convince me. I know you'll do what is right. So just go do it."

By the end of the month, I was able to return to work as an electrician. Gradually, I earned my way out of debt. At the same time, I grilled my brothers about their jobs. I bought books on the police department's test. I studied. And I applied to take the exam for police recruits. I scored well enough to be hired, but then was prevented from entering the Police Academy by a city-wide job freeze. Time went by and the limit on the hiring list expired.

Three years later I took the exam again, and shortly thereafter, I received a certified letter stating that my name had come up for hiring. *If I was still interested,* the letter said, I could report to the Police Academy on June 30, 1973, to begin the training that would convert me from a civilian to a member of the New York City Police Department.

Yes, I was still interested.

Five

MY first day, I arrived at the Police Academy on East Twentieth Street at 7:30 A.M. Behind a desk in the wide entrance lobby, the guard, a uniformed officer, hardly glanced at my letter of acceptance.

"Recruits in the first-floor gymnasium," he said, indicating a corridor with a slight gesture of his right thumb. And with a subdued thank you, I joined the swelling mass of other recruits from all over the five boroughs of New York City.

Since we were grouped by boroughs and then by zip codes as we proceeded through the lines, I was soon meeting others who would be coming in from Staten Island.

We were not allowed to bring cars, but were expected to ride public transportation. For all of us from Staten Island that meant two buses—which ran every half hour—just to get to the ferry depot, and then waiting for the ferry, which ran once an hour before dawn.

"We're going to get about four hours of sleep a night for the next six months," moaned Jimmy Sackel, the recruit in front of me.

"Not if we carpool," I said.

"That's against academy rules," a guy named Freddie Serio said. Another recruit named John Donoghue nodded in agreement.

"Somehow I can't see how riding the subways six hours a day, nine days a week, is going to make us better cops," I told them. "Besides, both my brothers did it. And they're on the force."

And so our carpool was born. And also, unfortunately, the four of us learned an initial lesson about NYPD rules: sometimes a petty deceit is the best way around a petty regulation.

Quickly we learned what we could and could not do as recruits and as probationary patrolmen.

We *could* make arrests, using a small green identification card that was issued the first week.

We could *not* carry a badge (or as cops call it, the "tin" or the "shield") or weapons of any sort. Arrests had to be made with our bare hands. The suspects were then turned over to anti-crime officers on active duty. Any such arrests by recruits would be carefully scrutinized by a review board.

And we could *not* use the elevators in the Police Academy for any reason. The elevators were reserved for the instructors while we hoofed it up and down seven flights of stairs throughout the summer and fall.

Our instructors were uniformed members of the police department, and they piled on a work load that was fully equivalent to a university curriculum, with police science courses as an extra.

English, math, and history. Psychology and political science. Criminal law. Business law. State law. City law. I had never known there was so much law until I was training to enforce it.

"Doesn't he know we got five other courses?" Eddie Ferretti whispered to me in class one day. Eddie, a good-looking, industrious kid from Staten Island, was quickly becoming a best friend.

"Sure, he knows," I responded. "It's just that he doesn't care."

Our poli sci instructor, who had the hearing of a guard dog, whirled around. "Someone have something to say?" he asked.

And of course no one peeped.

Then there was gym—five times a week, right in the middle of our class schedule. Down there in the first-floor gymnasium, there was no telling what to expect. Boxing. *("Lead with your right!")* Judo. *("The dropkick takedown can save your life!")* Water safety. *("Above all, gentlemen, do not drown in the department's swimming pool!")* Forty minutes of sit-ups, chins, jumping jacks, pull-ups, push-ups, standing broad jumps, and then maybe a mile run.

The gym was on the first floor, the day lockers were on the third floor, and the gym lockers were in the basement. We had fifteen minutes from the end of one period until the beginning of the next. And we couldn't use the elevators.

The intention, as those of us who survived eventually figured out, was to show us the frustrations and pressures of the job. The guy who lost his composure here washed out of the class. That's the way it had to be. How could anyone who couldn't hold his temper now be trusted out on the street with a shield and a revolver?

* * *

45

I got my first chance to be a real cop about three weeks after classes began. It was a Friday evening, and I had been to see a movie with some classmates—*The French Connection*. Yes, cops do go to cop movies.

I was alone in my car and about two minutes away from home when I pulled up at a red light. Hearing prolonged honking behind me, I turned and saw a green Pontiac with a man and a woman in it edging through the traffic. They were trying to attract the attention of a blue-and-white police patrol vehicle that had been at the head of the moving traffic. But as I looked up front again, I saw that the police car had already turned the corner. The Pontiac had made a little headway and was now next to me. I blew my own horn at them, rolled down my window, and called out, "What's the problem?"

The occupants were white, in their early twenties, and casually dressed. They appeared shaken.

"We were trying to get the police!" the driver shouted back.

I told them I was a cop, and again asked what was the matter.

"Her sister just got raped and robbed," the man said. "We're following the guy who did it. There!"

He pointed toward the intersection at Seaver Avenue, where I saw a figure striding briskly along the sidewalk.

"That's him!" the girl yelled. "That's him!"

The man was a white male, about five feet ten, also probably in his early twenties, with a strong broad-shouldered build. He was wearing dungarees and a yellow shirt.

"All right," I said. "Follow me."

I took off behind the man as he crossed Seaver Avenue and walked toward a boarding house on the north side of Oxford Place.

I followed him in my car while the other car kept behind me. The man entered the building, a standard New York City tenement. From the outside, I saw him walk up a flight of stairs and go into an apartment on the second floor.

While I watched, indignation won out over common sense. Only that morning, we had had Search and Seizure class at the academy. Two days earlier we'd brushed up on our judo. So what if my only weapons were my hands and a set of handcuffs, my only credentials a small green ID card bearing my eventual shield number?

I parked in front of the boarding house, clipped my handcuffs to my belt, and walked to the complainants' car, which was right behind mine. The light from the streetlamp was poor, but I could see them reasonably well. "Look," I said, "I'm going in there after this guy. I want you to call the police. Tell them what's going on. Then I'll meet you at the precinct."

"Which precinct?" the driver asked.

"The Hundred and twentieth in St. George," I said.

"Okay, officer. Will do," the man said.

"Officer," I thought to myself. It sounded so good I didn't bother to correct him. "Well, here goes. Got to make that first arrest sometime."

I walked up the stairs toward apartment 2-B. The door grew ever bigger as I approached.

I rang the bell. No answer. So I knocked. I waited. It was a warm night. My shirt was getting wet. I thought back to my Search and Seizure class that same day. I knew I couldn't enter the premises without a warrant.

"Hell, they're not going to invite me in," I said to myself. Then I thought about it. "Hmmm. Maybe they will."

There was no answer. So I knocked again.

"Hey! Open up in there!" I called out. I was sure that by now I was being watched by the neighbors through the peepholes of the surrounding doors.

Then the door to 2-B jerked open and a young Hispanic

47

man stood glowering before me wearing a soiled undershirt, shorts, and an expression that told me I wasn't welcome. He was about six feet tall. This was not the man I'd followed.

"Yeah?" he snarled. "Whadya want?"

"Hi, I'm Frankie's friend," I told him. "Frankie just came in here, didn't he?"

His expression changed. "Oh, yeah. You mean Pete, though, doncha?"

"Yeah, yeah," I said. "Pete. That's the guy. He's here, right?"

My new pal turned. "Hey Pete," he called to the apartment's other resident. "Some guy's out here to see you."

At that point I casually took half a step backward so that Pete would have to step into the hallway to see who his visitor was.

Pete was wary. He loomed in the doorway a few seconds later but safely inside. "I don't know this guy," he said, looking at me from a bad angle.

"Hey, Pete-boy," I laughed. "Come on, guy. We met two days ago. Don't you remember the business deal we were talking about?" I kept my hands where he could see them.

I gave him a big wide grin. Pete stood there frowning, with the door half open. I kept giving him the smile, even though I saw that he was concealing his right hand. This was the guy I wanted. I figured the hand concealed a knife.

"I don't know you," he said coldly.

"You're bullshitting me," I said.

The bare ceiling light was behind me so he had trouble seeing my face, which lured him into stepping a little farther out. He was near the doorway, then just past it and—

I lunged for him and grabbed his arm. Up it came. He pushed back and broke away from me, but I got between him and the doorway. His pal slammed the door.

There was a cold click and the glimmer of steel, even in that shadowy hallway. The guy had what's known as an "007" switchblade, the kind of street knife a cop most often sees.

"I'm a police officer," I said to him, giving him his chance. "I'm placing you under arrest."

"You ain't doing nothing, except getting cut," he said. He was about six feet away from me and angry as a wounded bear. He had the only weapon, but I knew what the academy had taught me and responded instinctively. When he came at me with that blade, holding it upright in his right fist and trying to slash it downward into my neck, I brought my own left hand straight up as hard as I could. If I could break his arm, fine. But the main thing was to knock that weapon away.

As he brought the knife down, I smashed his wrist with my forearm. Almost simultaneously, I stepped forward, thrusting my left leg behind his right one. I kicked my leg back in toward me, pulling his balance out from under him. We'd covered that move in gym class two days earlier. It had worked in rehearsal. It worked now.

The knife flew from his hand and the man dropped to the floor. He landed hard. The knife fell not far from his arm. I kicked it away with my foot, and then I pounced on the guy.

"Leggo of me, you bastard!" he yelled. "I ain't done nothing to you. Leggo! Leggo!"

Now, slowly at first, doors along the hallway began to open. The last thing I needed was an audience, particularly one that might sympathize with the suspect. While he went on screaming at me, I jerked his left hand behind his back and put the cuffs on his wrist. He flailed a punch toward me with the other hand, but then I pulled back his other arm until I had both wrists behind his neck and completed the cuffing procedure.

"Hey, whatdaya doin' to Pete?" a neighbor asked.

"Pete's under arrest," I said. "Robbery, assault, and rape."

"I ain't done nothing," Pete pleaded. "I been home all night."

"I followed you," I told him. I jerked him up to his feet. A belligerent crowd was beginning to gather, and I saw a very tall mocha-skinned man, who looked half-Spanish, half-Oriental, standing near the stairway, holding what appeared to be a broken baseball bat.

"You ain't no cop!" the man said to me. "Lemme see your gun and badge."

"I'm a cop, I'm a cop. Don't bother me."

"Pig! Fuck you!" one of the other neighbors said.

"Hey, he's a friend of mine. Let him go!" someone else shouted. "What are you comin' in here for grabbin' him?"

The best thing I could do for everyone was to get myself and my suspect out of there fast. I could deal with Pete. But a mob could kill me.

"I'm a cop!" I insisted. "And I'm taking this guy in." Holding my suspect by the arm, just above the elbow, I steered him toward the stairs. He was screaming the whole time, and giving some half-hearted resistance.

With the crowd now turning on me, I hustled Pete down the stairs and toward the front door. I hoped to see a police car waiting, but as I shoved my suspect out down the front steps, there was only the empty street. And the crowd had followed me out of the building onto the sidewalk.

I looked at my suspect. I looked at my car. I looked at the angry crowd that was closing in on me. And I began to feel very much alone.

"Okay, Pete," I said, directing him. "Get in the car!"

"Oh, no," he protested, starting to fight me again. "I ain't going—"

"In the car!" I repeated, slamming him into the back seat. Locking him in, I went around to the driver's side as the crowd circled us. Someone banged the hood. Someone else kicked the side door. A thrown bottle crashed nearby.

I gunned the engine. The crowd got the message and started to give way. Moments later they were safely behind us.

As I hauled my suspect into the precinct, the shifts were changing. The lieutenant on duty was named McNeely, a bespectacled, bushy-browed man in his forties with a lot of dark hair—a typical, cigar-chomping officer, who for years had booked arrests as they were dragged before his large elevated desk.

I stood in line behind a uniformed cop who was booking a guy for assault and a plainclothes detective who'd grabbed a suspect mugger. Both suspects were telling anyone nearby that their arresting officers, too, had the wrong guy.

Then it was my turn.

"Okay, officer," Lieutenant McNeely said to me. "What have you got?" I guess he took me for an off-duty cop who'd made a collar on the way home and brought the suspect to the nearest precinct. Standard procedure.

"One for rape, robbery, and assault," I began as I emptied my suspect's pockets onto the desk. The clerk inventoried each item. "Resisting arrest and assault on a police officer," I said. I plunked the 007 knife down onto the counter with just the proper amount of drama.

A small group of off-duty cops were watching the procedure. Watching what's getting booked is a favorite off-duty sport. Besides that, a man arrested for one thing may be wanted for several other crimes in the area. So it's always good police work to keep an eye on what's parading past the desk.

McNeely looked down at us through the haze of cigar smoke.

51

"Okay," he said gripping a ballpoint pen and starting to book it. "Who's the complainant?"

"They're on their way in, Lou," I said. (Anyone wearing lieutenant's bars in the police department is automatically called "Lou.") "They should be here in a few minutes."

He was still writing.

"All right, officer," he said. "What's your shield number?"

"Three one seven nine one," I said, giving the number of my green identification card.

"What's your command?"

"E.L.T.D."

The ballpoint came to a halt. Then he laid it aside and looked up sourly. "What's that? D.A.'s squad or some bullshit in Manhattan?"

"No, Lou. That's Entrance Level Training Division. Police Academy."

He'd started to write, but again his hand halted. He looked down at me with a stare of disbelief.

Other cops were now stopping to take in the show.

"You're a rookie," he said. "You don't have a gun or a shield?"

"That's right."

"What identification *do* you have?"

"I got a green card."

"What's a green card? You an alien or something?"

"No, sir. I'll show you what I mean."

Now I really had an audience. I pulled the green card out from my wallet and laid it on the desk.

At just that moment the complainants—the man and woman who'd flagged me down in the car, with the victim herself—arrived at the precinct. The victim turned out to have known her attacker, and identified him by name. "There he is. That's him!" she screamed, pointing to the suspect I had brought in.

As Lt. McNeely studiously handed me back my green card, two men approached. "Officer," one said, "I'm Detective Parisi. This is Detective Hearn. We'll take the collar on this man."

"You'll do what?" I said.

"We'll take the collar. This man is wanted for several other felonies." He flashed some papers, which turned out to be warrants for my suspect, plus his past record—a pedigree of sixty-ones, a series of robberies with felonious assault.

"The hell you will. He's mine," I said.

There was some whistles and chuckles from the audience, as the lieutenant ran a hand through his dark hair.

"Fox," he asked, "where'd you collar this guy?"

So I told my story.

"And all you had is this green card?" McNeely asked with disbelief.

"That's right, sir."

He blew a long stream of cigar smoke toward me, my suspect, the detectives, the victim, and her two friends, and delivered a long-suffering look. "Now look, Fox. I got to write out an unusual report. I got to send it over to your C.O. and have it on his desk by eight tomorrow morning. I got to assign one of my own men to safeguard your prisoner. And you got to appear in court and testify, at the expense of your classes. Now, don't you want the detectives to take this freak off your hands?"

"No, sir. He's my first collar."

"Okay, kid," he said. "You got him."

A week later, I made a second arrest, for drunken driving. Two days after that, I arrested a young man with a pistol.

Now, I wasn't out there looking for trouble. But I couldn't help being disturbed that so many people in New York had

53

already learned to look the other way. So if I saw something, I acted on it. Unfortunately I kept seeing things everywhere I looked.

Midway through my term at the academy, I had made twelve arrests. My classroom marks were somewhat less dramatic— about average or a little below. But I liked to think of myself as the type of guy who could be dropped into a situation and get the job done.

Of course, some people didn't see it quite that way. The academy was, after all, an academy. Grades were an essential part of the procedure. You had to have them to graduate. As rumors of my off-hours exploits circulated, most of them greatly exaggerated, I began to sound like some gung-ho psycho. One morning I asked my friends in the carpool to spread the word that I wasn't.

"But you are, Billy," Jimmy Sackel said. "You *are* gung-ho."

"And you *are* a psycho," Donoghue added.

"You're going to get us all in hot water," Serio admonished. "Why can't you control yourself until we graduate? Then you can go crack heads."

"Hey, these things happen to me," I protested.

"There's a dark cloud over this city," Donoghue intoned somberly. "And it follows you around, Chief."

Our time in transit was often spent needling each other or sharing the latest rumor. It helped ease the tensions of academy life. Each of us was scared for one reason or another that he wouldn't make it through. What we didn't realize at the time, of course, was how deeply we were all getting into the "cop syndrome." The jargon. The gossip. The hours. The dedication. We were adjusting our entire lives.

We weren't seeing the friends we used to see. We'd stopped

going to bars we'd once liked. In fact, many people didn't want to see us. We were part of the police force now. And cops make some people nervous.

Charlie's Bar usually had a little poker game going, so they wouldn't want someone like me subduing the atmosphere. Joey often had a few joints in his pocket, so he'd cross the street when he saw me coming. And Mrs. Leary, nice old Mrs. Leary whom I've known since I was a kid, had been buying cigarettes for years from a guy named Sal who got them at a great discount because they were bootlegged from North Carolina. So Mrs. Leary didn't want to talk anymore. Yes, I'd heard it would be a lonely job sometimes. But now it slowly dawned on me: the only individual one cop can completely trust is another cop.

Your professional life, your social life, your sex life, your family life, your church life—indeed your entire life—revolves around the fact that no one who doesn't wear the uniform fully understands. And once you start living the life of a cop, your enemies are the bad guys on the street, your friends are other police officers, and the rest are simply acquaintances.

I was engaged at the time to be married to a marvelous young woman named Mary Beth who developed a certain understanding of shifts, mandatory overtimes, and physical harm. But somewhere along the line I started paying more attention to the Academy than to her and she broke off our engagement. I wasn't surprised.

Nor could I really blame her.

In December, about two weeks before graduation, a city clerk came to the academy from downtown. He was a rumpled, ill-humored little man who looked like he'd spent too many years working for the city. He carried a cardboard box and a sheaf of official forms.

"The first thing I need from everybody in this room," he announced, "is twenty-five cents."

"For what?" Eddie Ferretti asked.

"For your safety pin," the clerk said.

It was with Mr. Begley's official New York City safety pin that an officer had to attach his shield to his chest. Nothing else would do. And once Mr. Begley had sold a pin to every recruit in Company 73-33, my graduating class, he started distributing the shields themselves, the tins that we would carry for our entire police careers.

"Auffredou, Linda," he called out. He dipped into his cardboard box and withdrew a small brown envelope as Linda Auffredou, one of the six women in our company, went forward to receive her shield and a crinkled batch of papers to sign.

There was no charge for the shield. It remained the property of the City of New York. The city could ask for it back at any time.

Linda Affredou returned to her seat and held her shining sheild in her hand. Those around her craned their necks to catch a glimpse of the first tin distributed among us. Mr. Begley continued through the names.

"Donoghue, John...Febles, Richard...Ferretti, Edward..."

The moment drew near.

"Fox, William Patrick..."

"Jesus. Even Fox gets a shield," said someone behind me.

"Sackel, James...Serio, Frederick..." And so on. But I wasn't listening anymore.

Three one seven nine one, I read, as I hefted the shield in

56

my hand. I liked the feel of it. I liked looking at it. I liked *having* it. I thought of my father, of how he'd struggled to take us upstate where the air was cleaner and where life might be better for his family. I thought of all those years he labored down in the dirty, unsafe trains that raced through the winding, damp tunnels beneath the city. His three boys had all become cops. I knew Dad would be pleased. Surprised, but pleased.

That afternoon, we all took the IRT down to police head-quarters at Center Street, where a property clerk in the base-ment handed each of us a heavy wooden box bearing a Smith & Wesson insignia.

"Don't open it," he instructed. "Take it back to the academy, get a receipt for it, and be at the firing range at Rodman's Neck tomorrow morning at eight."

And so the next morning I held my weapon in my hand for the first time. In the past, in the many hours I had spent at this range, I had used the department's firearms. But this was the one I had ordered, the one for which I had paid one hundred seventy-eight dollars.

Now I had to pass the test for the P.R.C., the Practical Revolver Course, with my own weapon. I would have to fire one hundred rounds from different positions. Unless I hit the target ninety-five times, I was still unqualified to be a cop.

Six recruits lined up on the range. We were given one hundred rounds of .38 caliber ammunition. We would be told when to shoot, how many rounds, and from what position. Part of the drill was to come out with the proper number of rounds fired. Heaven help the recruit who ran out of rounds too early or had a bullet left over.

"Ready on the firing line," the sergeant announced. *"Ready on the left. Ready on the right."*

Though I was confident of the outcome, my hands were slightly damp. Philosophically, this was not one of the pleasant parts of the job.

The target is in the unmistakable form of a human torso. There is no disguising what you are practicing to do. You are demonstrating your proficiency at shooting—and very possibly killing—another human being. Realistically, you *know* what a slug from a .38 caliber police special does. You know because you have seen it in the morgue. You know because you have heard the stories from older cops. Now you are showing how good you are at doing it. And, contrary to what many people believe, we do not practice to wing the arms or hit the legs. We are instructed to aim at the largest part of the target and to hit it.

"I hope to God I never have to do this for keeps," I thought to myself, eye to eye with my target.

"Standing position, weapon supported," the sergeant ordered. "Load five rounds."

We drew our weapons from their holsters. We loaded.

"Commence firing!"

The room was filled with a series of deafening blasts from our pistols. Firing all at once, we sounded like a small guerrilla band. I squeezed off my five shots, holding my supported hand as steady as possible. The gun was ugly and powerful in my hand. The barrel flashed and a cloud of smoke was suddenly everywhere.

"Unload, lock and reload six rounds," the sergeant instructed. "Keep it moving. Police crouch next. Fire six rounds. Move back to twenty yards."

We continued to fire. Round after round slid into the cylinder of the pistol and then erupted from the barrel. Standing. Crouching. Weapon supported by one's other hand, weapon unsupported. And so on. There was no easing up. This was the final exam. I watched the little round holes blow out of the blackness of the target. Ten yards. Twenty yards. Thirty yards away.

Then it was over. I came out with the right number of rounds. We holstered our weapons and any spent shells that had fallen we placed in a bucket. Today, every bit of brass gets recycled.

"Good shooting, Fox," the sergeant said a few minutes later. "At twenty yards I believe you could shoot the gonads off a flea."

"Then I passed?"

"You got a ninety-eight, officer. Take the weapon home with you."

On December 9, the department posted the assignments for academy graduates. I groaned when I saw them. I had drawn the Tenth Precinct, a comparatively quiet stretch of Manhattan's Lower West Side. I longed instead for the hotter "action" precincts like the Forty-second in the South Bronx, the Twenty-eighth on Manhattan's Upper West Side or the Sixty-seventh in central Brooklyn.

But I had little time to grieve. Graduation was two days later at the Seventh Regiment Armory, Park Avenue and Sixty-eighth Street. Mayor Lindsay was there. So were Controller Abe Beame and the Police Commissioner Donald Cawley. At the end of the ceremony as we stood and took our oath, I felt what every man and woman in that room must have felt before and after me: the bond of the blue uniform. We were now different from everyone else.

Six

MICHAEL

AT the hospital, Michael was given a number of psychological tests. He asked why he kept having to lie on a couch and talk to these doctors. They said they were trying to help him. And they wanted to find him a new home, a better one than he'd ever known.

"What if my dad comes back?" Michael asked one of the nurses.

"He's got two years," she reassured him. "Maybe he'll use the time to solve his own problems."

"Maybe," Michael said without expression. He thought about it as he watched the nurse. She was a woman in her early thirties with a thin figure, reddish blond hair, and an attractive face. "What if he never comes back?" he asked finally.

Her face melted into a sympathetic smile, and she gave the

boy a slight hug. "Oh, Michael," she said. "Every man wants a son. I'm sure he'll be back when he can."

Two weeks later Michael was placed in a foster home. Things started to work out. Frank Dolan and his wife Evelyn had always wanted a son. They had two little girls younger than Michael and took him in.

Frank Dolan was a career man in the United States Navy. He was an intelligence officer and a good one. In his uniform he looked right out of a movie. The Dolans lived in Millington, Tennessee, on the naval air station, just outside Memphis. Michael enjoyed being a navy brat. He had family and friends and he did well in school.

But there was a problem, bedwetting, whenever Michael got scared or lonely. Once in the car when the Dolan family was going somewhere, Michael had this problem. His foster father made him stay in the car while the family went shopping.

When they returned, Frank Dolan placed a hand on Mike's shoulder. "You're too old for that sort of thing, Michael," he said. "Let's make that the end of it."

The problem didn't happen again.

After a year and a half, the Dolans filed papers with the state of Tennessee to move for permanent adoption. Michael would complete the family. Everyone was pleased. Then there was the terrible day in April 1975.

Michael knew something was wrong when his father met him after school with the car. Michael climbed into the front seat. They started to drive.

"Hey, Dad," Michael asked. "What's wrong?"

Frank Dolan pulled the car over to the side of the road. "I got my orders today," he said. "I'm being transferred to San Diego."

"Hey, great!" Michael said. "When do we leave?"

Frank Dolan sadly looked the boy in the eye. "Immediately," he said softly. "But I'm afraid Child Welfare won't let you come with us."

There was a silence within the car. "What do you mean?" Michael said. "You moved for legal adoption."

"Your father still has time to come back and take you with him. He has another six months."

"But he moved out West!" Michael persisted. "No one even knows where he is. He hasn't made support payments and—"

Frank Dolan took the boy's hand. "I know, Michael," he said. "I know it's not fair. But Child Welfare won't let you leave the State of Tennessee with us."

"But—"

"It's all decided, Michael," Frank Dolan said. "I've been on the telephone with them all day. The law is the law."

Michael began to cry. He couldn't speak. His foster father pulled the car back onto the road.

"You come home and we'll help you pack up," he said. "The social worker wants you back tomorrow morning. I'm sorry, son. I don't make the regulations."

The next morning the social worker came. She was very understanding and Michael was very upset. She moved him into an institution for a few days and then tried several more foster homes. But Michael didn't like any of them.

Michael was moved into a home with twenty other boys and he didn't like that, either. The boys fooled around a lot in the showers, bad stuff that terrified him. He got into fights. He didn't have any friends. One day a kid punched him in the mouth and he lost two front teeth.

A Mormon family took him in for a while with a number of other foster children but this went so badly that Michael ran away on a cold night, hid near the river, and nearly froze.

62

From Lakeside Hospital he went to another home where there were six foster children. The parents received $175 per month per child and the father drank. The mother was seldom there and the refrigerator was nearly always empty.

Michael ran away again but didn't get far. He was found in the bus terminal and returned.

Discovering a can of lighter fluid in the garage, Michael squirted the fluid onto the living room draperies, and put a match to them. Though he doused the flames himself, the social workers decided to try another sort of place for Michael—The Tennessee Psychiatric Hospital for Children in Memphis.

Michael stayed at this hospital for several months. It was a pretty good place.

One day a couple in their fifties came to meet Michael. Mr. and Mrs. James Forrest were both teachers who didn't have children of their own. They took Michael into their home and things went quite well for a while.

The Forrests' neighbors were in their fifties or sixties. Elderly, Michael considered them. They hired Michael to cut lawns after school and on weekends. He earned as much as twenty-five dollars a week and on Saturdays his foster father would take him to the movies. Things worked out for about a year and a half.

Then Mr. Forrest was assigned new duties at a new school and things changed. Mr. Forrest started inviting boys over and organized football games for them. The boys were mostly black, bigger than Michael, and Michael was not asked to play.

One Saturday Michael ran away. The police brought him back two days later, scared and crying. Mr. Forrest tried to understand but he always seemed involved with others.

The next time Michael went to the top of the Sears Tower

by himself. He had no intention of jumping. He just wanted someone to listen. But the police took him down and brought him to juvenile court for causing a disturbance. Mr. Forrest sadly said that he just couldn't handle him anymore. The boy didn't seem like a bad kid. But such a constant troublemaker for a thirteen-year-old.

Michael shuttled back and forth between the John S. Wilder Youth Development Center and another series of foster homes. Nothing worked out. There was more bedwetting. There was another small fire. One day he took a long walk that ended up at the airport.

A flight was arriving. As people disembarked, Michael slipped through the gates and mingled with the passengers. Then he worked his way back toward the plane, ran up to two stewardesses, and flashed his biggest smile.

"Ma'am, I left my luggage. Can I go back on?"

The stewardess asked, "Do you remember where your bags were?"

"Yes, ma'am."

"Go ahead," she said.

Michael boarded the plane and locked himself in a washroom. After takeoff, he found a seat. Six hours later he was in Los Angeles where, not knowing what else to do, he repeated the trick and landed in Honolulu.

In Hawaii, he met a girl named Christine. She lived on the streets and was a shoplifter. They now practiced together. As Christine distracted sales clerks, record albums went down Mike's pants or up his shirt. Rings would go onto his fingers or into his mouth. Watches went around the ankles. They fenced their take to teenagers on the street.

One day Christine was sick, so by himself, Michael returned to a store that had always been easy. He was halfway out the door with a leather tote bag under his coat when a security guard grabbed him. Half an hour later, he was in police custody.

"Look, you can't arrest me," Michael pleaded tearfully. "My father's in the Navy. It'll hurt his career."

"In the Navy where?" a robbery detective asked. "Here?"

The detective picked up the telephone and called the Military Police at Pearl Harbor. Michael told them the same story. A check of personnel records in Hawaii deflated Michael's tale.

A day later the Wilder Center received a collect call from Hawaii. Michael had set a Center record for the farthest any runaway had ever traveled. But the Wilder Center was still legally responsible for him and paid to fly him back to Memphis. There they were greatly relieved to turn him over to juvenile court and thus be rid of him.

Seven

O N the Saturday morning I reported for my first assignment, the desk sergeant at the Tenth Precinct was a ruddy, square-shouldered bear of a man named Ken Kosko. The moment I arrived, I dropped some completed forms on his desk, then toed the line like an arrestee as he unfolded them.

"What the hell's this?" he grunted.

"Request for a transfer, sergeant," I told him.

His eyes shifted down in the squinting, dyspeptic long-suffering glare that sergeants have turned into an art form.

"You being a wise-ass?" he asked. "You're a rookie. You don't put in for a transfer the minute you walk in here. You don't even know what this place is like."

"I did my homework," I said. "I got two brothers on the job. North of here, the Two-oh and the Two-four are hot houses. South of here, the Six and the Nine are heavies. Midtown North and Midtown South are prestige houses and west of us is the Hudson River. That's Harbor Patrol, which is Special Operations. I need five years of high-crime experiences to get into Special Operations. So I want to move."

"Well, you can move your ass upstairs. Your three-day orientation program is starting in five minutes."

Upstairs, seven uniformed officers who were also new to the precinct were sitting, waiting, in the squad room. I sat down next to my friend Eddie Ferretti, one of the few familiar faces in the house.

A Lieutenant Sanders soon entered the room and began telling us about the Tenth Precinct. Our boundaries were Fourteenth Street north to Forty-second, Eighth Avenue to the Hudson River. We had Chelsea, the garment district, the lower edge of Times Square, part of the theater district, the General Post Office, the old Pennsylvania Railroad yards, the wholesale meat markets, and the Port Authority.

Chelsea was quiet and mostly residential, Lt. Sanders told us. Muggers worked the area but not very often since it was a long run to the uptown Eighth Avenue subway. The General Post Office at Thirty-third Street was occasionally a target for robbers, but the Post Office had their own federal guards. They didn't need us very often. The railroad yards were a popular dumping ground for murder victims since many of the tracks entered tunnels that ran for several blocks. No big problem there since the corpses became the headache of the homicide division. The Port Authority was a popular stomping ground for prostitutes who inevitably drew crime into the area. Anyone who got mugged or ripped off on the south side of Forty-second Street was in our territory. The north side belonged to the Midtown North Precinct. But if we saw anything, poaching was permitted.

"You'll find," said the lieutenant as he motioned on a map

of the area across Forty-second Street, "that this area is our biggest trouble spot."

Still using the map, he moved on. "We got a lot of gay bars down toward Fourteenth Street," he said, "and a lot of middle-class gays living in Chelsea. Now, you have to be careful with them. They can be touchy, same as any other minority group, and you'll get called in to arbitrate fights between them." He rolled his eyes. "Now, don't smirk. You treat them same as any other citizen. But if you get called into a gay bar for any problem, request a back-up team right away. Otherwise, you can get the whole crowd turning on you."

After we had been shown around the precinct house so we'd know where everything was, we were given the grand tour of our territory by car. The next morning, a Sunday, we went out on our own.

Climbing into the uniform that Sunday for the first time, knowing I was going to go out on patrol, be my own boss, and deal with the public as a New York City police officer was one of the highs of my life. But I could not forget that I was in a residential neighborhood in the West Twenties, among blocks of restored townhouses and small brick apartment buildings—clean, prosperous, orderly, and quiet.

I returned to the precinct at lunch hour and handed Sgt. Kosko another request for a transfer.

I had been in the Tenth Precinct for one week when I heard screams and saw a Greyhound bus moving south on Ninth Avenue with a crowd chasing it. Then I saw a red trail coming from beneath the bus.

I ran out into the traffic on Ninth Avenue, my hands upraised. Cars swerved around me. The tires of the bus squealed as the vehicle screeched to a sudden stop.

"A woman!" someone screamed.

I had known since I accepted my shield that a moment like this was coming. But how can you prepare for the sight of an elderly woman, her body twisted by the filthy underpinnings of a seven-ton bus? One of her legs was severed at the knee. The other was folded in an impossible direction, blood flowing freely from the joint.

I prayed silently as I crawled beneath the bus and used part of her coat to staunch the wounds. I grabbed the police walkie-talkie at my belt and called for a unit of the New York City Police Emergency Squad. Then I called my precinct to ask for an ambulance and a doctor.

A Port Authority policeman named John Faugno crawled under the bus to say that a doctor had generously stepped out of the crowd. By the time Faugno, the doctor, and I had applied tourniquets to her legs, the Emergency Services van had arrived, followed by an ambulance, and the woman was soon on her way to Bellevue.

This entire sequence of events had taken less than twenty minutes. The doctor identified himself as Norman Pastarek of New Rochelle. The victim's name was Lucienne Houlot. I learned later that she had lost both legs. But after extensive surgery, she survived.

When I passed Sgt. Kosko in the lunch room a few days later, he said "Good police work, kid. You saved a life out there."

Sgt. Kosko kept me moving around the precinct on foot patrol for several weeks. After that, I was assigned to two-man teams in a patrol car.

I worked a lot with Eddie Ferretti. But my very first partner was an experienced officer named Bill Sportiello, who, I'd heard, some guys didn't like to work with.

"How come?" I asked.

"Work a shift with him and you'll find out."

And so I did. Sportiello's nickname, given affectionately, was "Motormouth." He was like a twenty-four-hour news station. I didn't mind. He knew the precinct well and played the game like a good cop. That was more important.

A curious assignment those days concerned the G & D Escalator Maintenance Company on Eleventh Avenue. As well as supposedly attending to the occasional broken elevator, G & D was known to be the legal front for an organized crime family. Patrol cars in our sector were instructed to keep an eye on the place. So if nothing was doing elsewhere, we might drive by to see what was double-parked out front. Sometimes we'd ticket the double-parkers and enjoy the thought that perhaps we'd hung a summons on some Mafia bigshot.

A more serious aspect of the work involved noting the license plate of any visitor to G & D. We would then call Central on a ten fifteen, a verification request, and have the plate number run through a computer deep in the heart of police headquarters. Seconds later a return call would place the license in one of three categories:

Ten sixteen was a stolen car.
Ten seventeen, the car was clean—neither stolen nor yet connected to organized crime.
Ten eighteen, the car was registered in the name of someone known to consort with mobsters or was tied to a New York crime family.

If we had a stolen car, a ten sixteen, we were onto something that fell into the category of Grand Larceny–Auto, and we'd turn it over to the precinct's Auto Theft Squad. If we had a ten eighteen, we'd established the whereabouts of a known mobster. And if the car had previously been completely clean, a ten seventeen, we had established a new bit of information.

Sometimes these people leaving G & D would see us and wave. We'd wave back. Might as well be friendly. But what was this, I wondered at first. A grown-up game of cops and robbers?

Well, yes it was. These organized crime guys planned to break the law and considered it our job to catch them. A mobster didn't shoot a cop in the back and we didn't bust a mob member without a reason. Each side knew the unwritten rules and, in a strange way, played by them.

One night I was working in a sector car with veteran cop Charlie Madsen when a panel truck swerved past. I saw that it carried the G & D logo. After the truck had barrelled through two red lights, we decided to give it a tail.

Sixty seconds later, we'd pulled it over. The driver, a teen-age Hispanic, tried to flee. But Madsen tackled him a block away. It seemed that the garage of G & D had been broken into. And we had ourselves an arrest for Grand Larceny–Auto, what's known as a "good" collar.

While Officer Madsen took the kid to Central Booking, I went back to the precinct and filled out the appropriate arrest forms. If G & D was as dubious a concern as I'd been led to believe, I wondered, how long would they let one of their panel trucks sit in the Tenth Precinct parking lot?

By then it was nearly midnight.

A few mintues past 1 A.M. as I was changing into civilian clothing to go home, the property clerk gave me a call. A lawyer for G & D Escalator had come to claim the truck.

In the property clerk's office a little man with a weasel face and bags under his eyes was waiting with all the proper registration and ownership papers for the truck. The clerk, Sgt. Jerry Royce, introduced him as Nat Goldman.

"Officer Fox here made the collar on the youth who stole your truck," Sgt. Royce told him.

Goldman looked up at me with a thin smile, and grunted something.

"You're pressing charges, I hope," I said. "Against the kid we arrested."

"No. No charges, officer," he said quietly. "We just want to get our truck back."

"Must be an important truck," I said.

He looked at me coldly. "All our property is important. We're a small company. We have trouble surviving in the city. We can't afford to lose a truck."

"Well, the company must be doing pretty well to afford a lawyer who'll jump out of bed at 1 A.M. to come in to claim a stolen truck."

Goldman gave me another thin smile. "I'm here as a favor to my clients," he said. He turned back to Sgt. Royce. "Are we finished?" he said.

Royce completed the forms. Goldman was given the keys to his truck and told he could drive it away.

I had no legal right to examine the truck or do any search. But when Goldman returned to the parking lot, I was walking slowly around his truck, checking the tires, just giving it the once over. He looked very tired as he walked to the driver's side and unlocked the door.

"Anything wrong, officer?" he asked.

"Nope." I gave him my big friendly smile.

"Then I'll be on my way," he said.

He opened the cab door. As he went to pull it shut, I placed my hand on the frame.

72

"I was just thinking," I said. "That kid went to a lot of trouble to steal one of your trucks. Why do you suppose he did that?"

"I have no idea," he said.

"There are plenty of vans parked on the street. Why did he want to rip you off?"

"I have no idea," he said again.

He tried to close the door, but I held it.

"I'd really like to find out," I said. "Mind if I go back to your garage with you and look around?"

His face whitened.

"I *do* mind," he said.

"Why?"

"Officer," he said, "I'm very tired. It's the middle of the night. I have to be in my office in six hours and I haven't had any sleep.

"Some nights are like that," I commiserated. "But why don't I just drive over with you and have a quick look."

After a long stare, as if realizing that I knew more about the company he represented than might be healthy for his clients, he was suddenly very friendly. Reaching for a piece of paper on the dashboard, he wrote something on it. "You've done your work well tonight, officer," he said. "My company is appreciative, of course. If you'd ever like us to do you a favor, just give us a call."

He handed me the paper. It listed a man named Frankie and gave a telephone number.

I let him close the door to the van and drive off, thinking he had made me happy.

Back indoors I wrote up a report on the conversation to the precinct's intelligence division and enclosed the slip of paper.

*   *   *

Sportiello and I were on patrol in the Twenties when the division radio told us that there was a reported dispute on West Seventeenth Street between Fifth and Sixth Avenues. We were five blocks to the west. We said we'd take it.

Then the radio crackled more ominously.

"THAT'S A TEN TEN," Central said. "MAN WITH A GUN. POSSIBLE SHOTS FIRED."

It belonged to the Thirteenth Precinct. But poaching was allowed, and it was also a serious enough call for any available car to respond.

Crossing Sixth Avenue at Seventeenth Street, I saw there was a crowd halfway up the block. My heart started to pump hard and I could see the intent look on Sportiello's face. Walking or driving into a situation involving an armed man is treacherous. The first gunman you see could be an undercover cop, an off-duty cop, an F.B.I. agent, or a private guard. You have a second or two to act. Then you have a lifetime to live with the outcome of that decision.

Now I saw there was a lone man on the south side of the block, glaring and shouting at a crowd of about twenty agitated people across the street who were cursing back at him.

I tried to see if there was a racial angle to the situation. I didn't see one. The crowd was mixed. The lone man was white. But I had trouble seeing him clearly because of the parked cars on his side of the street. Then he moved slightly and I saw the reflection off something in his hand.

"He's got a gun," I said sharply to Sportiello. "Let me out."

My partner eased the car to a halt. I jumped out and the patrol car continued to creep forward. I moved to the side of the street where the gunman was and I drew my weapon. I advanced on the man carefully. He was still watching the crowd across the street, shouting at them. He hadn't seen me.

By now I had made dozens of arrests, but I had yet to fire

my weapon at another human being. With all my thoughts, fears, and instincts jammed into one or two seconds, I advanced to within twelve feet of the man's left side. He still hadn't seen me.

Sportiello had now left the patrol car and aimed his weapon at the man from cover. I aimed mine at him, too.

"Police officer!" I shouted. "Freeze!"

But he didn't freeze. Jolted, he whirled toward me. With the crowd beginning to scream, he moved his gun upward into a firing position, took aim at my chest and pulled the trigger.

I heard a nerve-shattering *click*. He had tried to kill me and his gun had jammed. I felt the big empty flash of mortality within my chest, right where the bullet would have gone.

"Drop it!" I screamed, my finger tight on the trigger of my own weapon. But he didn't drop it and suddenly I was hurtling forward. I have never covered twelve feet so quickly in my life.

I crashed into him shoulder first, knocking him clear across the sidewalk. A long obscene grunt rose from his throat, while the pistol flew from his hand.

With a leap through the parked cars, Sportiello was at my side. He recovered the pistol. Still in a fury, I picked up the gunman and threw him against a wall.

"Easy, Bill," I heard Sportiello saying. "You got him. You got him."

I arranged him against the wall, forcing his hands up for a frisk. It was not the gentlest toss I'd ever done. Moments later, I had the cuffs on him as other patrol cars began arriving. The recognition of what had happened would stay with me for months.

Sportiello was at my side. "Why didn't you shoot him?" he asked.

"I didn't want to shoot," I heard myself answering. "I don't

know. I didn't want to shoot. One of those things. I just didn't."
I turned to him. "Why didn't *you* shoot?" I asked.

"Couldn't," Sportiello replied, motioning to the lobby of the building directly behind the gunman. A group of people, he indicated, had been trapped there. "Might have hit a civilian," he explained.

"Yeah," I said absently. "Don't want to hit a bystander."

A sergeant from the One-three came up and placed a hand on my shoulder. "You okay?" he asked.

"I'm all right," I nodded.

"Should have blown the dumb fucker away," the sergeant grumbled. "Would have saved the city a lot of trouble."

Sportiello held the chrome-plated forty-five that had nearly been the instrument of my execution. I looked at it with a shudder. It was a fine weapon, expensive and carefully crafted. My partner examined it. A bullet had been chambered. The weapon was ready to fire. Sportiello removed the clip and the ammunition. The sergeant took the empty pistol, aimed it at the sidewalk and pulled the trigger. It clicked.

"You're a lucky son of a bitch, officer," he said. "Nothing mechanical wrong with this piece. Would have made a hole in your chest the size of a watermelon."

The man who tried to kill me was a Vietnam veteran. He had been visiting the city from North Carolina and had brought an illegal handgun with him. As he sat in the apartment of friends, some kids outside bounced a ball against the building. When the ball went wild and broke a window, the man had thought he was under fire.

His response was to threaten the crowd across the street—and to fire when confronted by a police officer.

For this, the man received a two-year sentence. Eighteen

months of it was immediately suspended. Most of the rest was reduced for good behavior. So the judge in the case eventually let the man off with time served—three weeks at Rikers Island—and the defendant agreed to leave New York City after his hearing.

We both got off lucky.

Eight

UNTIL the day Mayor Beame gave his state-of-the-city address on January 1, 1975, he had been popular with the police department, primarily because he had compaigned on a pledge to hire five thousand new officers.

But after a year in office, he saw the city was going to have to start tightening payroll. So when the five hundred recruits currently in the Police Academy had completed their studies, they were to be "furloughed."

"That little bastard!" muttered a veteran named Ken O'Malley who stood near me in the locker room of the ten house on a cold January morning. "Beame knew all along there would never be money for five thousand new cops. It's just another example of the politicans fucking us over." There was no particular bitterness in O'Malley's voice. To him, it was routine.

The younger guys liked to hear O'Malley bitch but didn't

necessarily take him seriously. A house just wouldn't be right without a few resident soreheads. Yet on this particular point, O'Malley's views were not at odds with the common feeling on the force.

"And I'll tell you something else," O'Malley continued as he pulled on his bullet-proof vest. "Today they screw the recruits by not giving them jobs. Tomorrow they screw us by giving us layoffs."

"There have never been any layoffs in the history of the department," I reminded him.

"There's always a first," he muttered. "I'm just glad I've got eleven years of seniority. Before you know it we'll be replaced by postal employees." He looked at me. "How much time you got on the force, Fox? You at another house before you came here?"

"I started the academy in June of seventy-three."

"You're a goner," he said. He looked up. "You, too, Ferretti. You better learn how to jerk sodas for a living."

That brought Eddie reluctantly into the conversation. "Know why they'll never lay off a cop?" Eddie asked.

"Tell us," O'Malley challenged, hoisting his gun belt around his waist and buckling it. "I would truly like to know."

"They can't lay off a single cop because every other cop in the city will go on strike as a show of sympathy."

"Bullshit, man," O'Malley declared. "You can't strike in this blessed line of work. Against the Taylor Law, remember? Every guy on this force signed a pledge not to strike." O'Malley clipped his shield onto his blue shirt.

"The same Taylor Law promises us employment," I shot back. "We agree not to strike only if the city promises us employment after our one year probationary period."

"Sorry, gents," O'Malley concluded, "but if they decide to

stick it to you, they will. Now, excuse me. I got to go to work."

Eddie gave me a look as O'Malley sauntered away.

"What do you think?" he asked.

"It'll never happen," I told him confidently.

By late that spring, I had put in more than fifteen months on the job. I felt I belonged there. But I was still haunted by O'Malley's words.

The graduates of the Academy had *not* received jobs. And as the City of New York struggled in red ink, the idea of layoffs in the uniformed services—Police, Fire, and Sanitation—did not seem as remote a threat. Our union, the P.B.A., had been offered a generous concession: every cop in the department would work five days with no pay in order to ease the burden on the city's payroll; in exchange, we'd received a promise that no one would be furloughed. The offer was accepted and the promise was made by the mayor's office.

At about three o'clock one afternoon I was in the precinct getting ready for an evening shift. Lieutenant Sanders walked by my locker and placed a hand on my shoulder. "You got a visitor." he said.

"Who is it?" I asked.

"F.B.I.," he said. "Two of them."

They were waiting in a small interrogation room on the second floor—two polite, short-haired, straight-arrow types in gray suits, white shirts, and dark neckties. They introduced themselves as members of a joint federal-city strike force on organized crime. They were Special Agents Edward Caproni and Matthew Daley.

Reviewing a series of dossiers concerning corruption in various industries in Manhattan, Brooklyn, and Staten Island, they had found the report I'd filed the night the van was stolen from G & D Escalator Repair.

The "Frankie" whom Nat Goldman had been trying to put me in touch with, Caproni explained, was known to be a "soldier" in one of the five Manhattan crime families.

"Not the type of guy a cop wants to hang out with," I suggested.

"On the contrary," Caproni replied. "Frankie may think you'd be useful to him."

"As what?" I answered, my indignation perfectly apparent.

"As his eyes and ears in this precinct," Caproni said. "He probably wants to see how corruptible you are."

"Not very."

"Of course," Caproni said. "But suppose Frankie thinks you are. Suppose you were one of the officers caught in the upcoming layoffs. What if—"

"I don't want any part of a layoff," I told them quickly.

"We're just 'supposing,'" Daley soothed. "We're just talking things out."

"Suppose you were laid off from this department," Caproni said. "That might make it appear you have an ax to grind against your former employer. Suppose you then went to Frankie to see what he could do for you."

I was silent.

"He might be receptive," Daley suggested.

I knew they had done their homework on me. I was certain they had spoken to my commanding officer.

"Why don't you tell me what you're getting at?" I asked.

They exchanged glances and Daley gave Caproni a slight nod.

"We might want you to go undercover," Caproni said to me. "You'd be in a dangerous situation, no doubt about that.

You'd have no shield, no weapon, and no identification as a police officer. You'd be known to the strike force and to commanding officers of the involved precincts in the city. Aside from that, no one would know you."

I listened hard, wondering whether I'd taken a wrong turn and ended up on a set for *Serpico*.

"Your sergeants spoke highly of you," Daley said in seductive tones. "They said you like to be where the action is."

"Yeah, but this isn't exactly what I had in mind. I like wearing the uniform."

"Of course," said Caproni. "But this is another way you can be useful. You might be able to establish a line on some of the filthiest racketeers in the city."

I turned it over.

What these guys were offering me was a chance to strike a blow at some of New York's homegrown scum. Or a chance to get my head blown off.

"And you think I might be good because I've got no wife and kids," I said. "So if I get killed, I'm the only one who's out."

Caproni shrugged, as if to admit that I had a point.

Daley spoke. "You don't have to do it."

"When would it be?" I asked.

Now Daley shrugged. "We don't know," he said. "We just wanted to sound you out. In case you were still bored in this precinct."

"We've counted twenty-three transfer applications," Caproni said. "So what do you think? Are you interested?"

"When you want me," I said, "give me a call."

The last week of June, the mayor and the governor bullied the state legislature into passing a piece of legislation that would pay unemployment compensation to members of the Fire, Police, and Sanitation departments, men who under the law could not be laid off, but were about to be laid off anyway.

Personnel changes always come down on a Friday or a Monday so they can be worked into precinct charts. The changes—such as a transfer from one precinct to another—come via the teletype terminals at each precinct and at headquarters. Somehow we'd gotten past Friday, June 27, without the ominous clatter of the teletype. But at 1 P.M. on June 29, the ticker sprang to life. I was working that day. There was a Gay Liberation Day parade from Greenwich Village up Seventh Avenue to Central Park. Some of the men from our precinct were assigned to do parade duty along Seventh Avenue. I was among them. The parade was an orderly one with very few incidents. But early in the afternoon, I heard the rumor: There were so many terminations coming through that the teletype had begun a day early.

"The ticker is jumping off the table," Ed Yarrow from Midtown South came by and told me. "They're axing us."

"How many?" I asked. With only eighteen months of seniority on the force I knew I had cause to worry.

"The ticker's been going for an hour and a half," the cop said. "It shows no signs of stopping."

"An hour and a half?" I repeated. "Jesus Christ! How many men could they be terminating?"

He looked me in the eye. "Want to hear the rumor from downtown? Four thousand," Yarrow said.

There was no reply. I knew a figure like that meant that all the men hired for the last five years would be losing their jobs. When I returned to the precinct after my shift, the place was like a morgue.

There was a crowd around the teletype. Some men who had

83

already seen their names sat on isolated wooden chairs or stared blankly out the grimy windows. Others had their faces in their hands. Some wept.

Sergeants and lieutenants walked around offering fatherly words of encouragement. An officer named Dennis Rogers who'd graduated from the academy about six months before I had said to me softly, "You know, last November my wife stopped working. We figured I was secure here. She's having a baby in two months. Now what?"

"I don't know, Denny," I said. "Something's got to turn up. Something's got to."

I walked to the teletype. Sgt. Kosko and Denny O'Mally stood grimly watching it. Sgt. Kosko turned and saw me for the first time. I didn't have to ask.

"Don't bother to look, Bill," he said. "You're gone. So is Ferretti and so are seven others from this house. Thus far."

I stayed at the precinct until the bitter end, sinking deeper and deeper into an angry depression. By seven o'clock that evening both of my brothers had turned up on the list. My brother-in-law, Mike O'Connell, got axed about ten.

Shortly after one o'clock the teletype fell silent. Its day's work was over. No fewer than five thousand men and women had been wiped out of the police department in a single twelve-hour period. No firings for a hundred and fifty years—then five thousand in a day.

The minority hiring program was obliterated. Most of the women officers who had recently been hired were terminated. My entire class from the academy was gone, as was every other class for the last five years. The only exceptions were those who had served in Vietnam. Their military service, for some reason, would count as time served in the department.

Otherwise the computer had been merciless. It even terminated a cop named Angel Poglio, who two months earlier had been half blinded by a bomb planted in East Harlem by Puerto Rican nationalists.

"Just tell me this," Denny O'Malley asked, "who's going to protect the city?"

On Monday morning I rose at my usual time, drove to the Tenth Precinct and parked my car in the lot. The precinct was as still as death. Of 196 men assigned to the ten house, 34 had been furloughed.

Sgt. Patrick Greer, the property clerk, sat at a desk with Police Officer James McGullough beside him while the victims of the purge lined up before them. When my turn came, I placed my two weapons on the desk and slid them toward the sergeant.

"That's one Smith and Wesson .38 caliber military-type revolver," I said flatly. "Serial number D 5356787. And one Smith and Wesson .38 caliber Chief revolver, off duty, serial number 850J8."

Sgt. Greer and Officer McGullough inventoried the two weapons, and handed me a receipt. I watched them write. These guys were my friends. They could barely look us in the eye. They were as angry and disgusted as we were.

"Your summons book?" the sergeant asked.

I handed in my summons book, my patrol guide (known as "The Bible"), my department helmet, my department identification card, and two boxes of .38 caliber ammunition.

"I'm sorry, Bill," Sgt. Greer said. "I can't help thinking everyone will be back tomorrow. I can't see how they can do this."

"Who's going to stop them?" I asked.

He shook his head in disgust.

"There's a rally down at City Hall tomorrow," McGullough said. "Everyone's going to be there."

"I'll be with everyone," I said.

I knew no one behind me was anxious to reach that desk, so I took a moment to scan the room.

I thought back to the two exams I'd taken to get this job. Then I thought of the electrical work I'd done. I could have had my own business by this time, I told myself. But no, I'd wanted to help people. I'd wanted to be a cop.

"Forgetting something, aren't you?" Sgt. Greer asked gently.

"Oh. Yeah. Sorry," I said. I reached to my back pocket and pulled out my shield case. Flipping it open, I undid the city's twenty-five cent safety pin and removed shield number three one seven nine one from the leather case. I placed it respectfully on the desk in front of me. And left.

The next afternoon, when five hundred angry former cops turned up at City Hall with an equal number of dismissed fire fighters and sanitation workers, the mayor and the president of our union were out of town.

We assembled behind police barricades and chanted frustration at the mayor's office and at the City Council. When we tried to move forward, we were met by a line of uniformed officers. It was eerie. Had we not been laid off, we would have been on the other side. Guys we knew, guys we had worked with, guys we had risked our lives for, stood with their nightsticks ready.

Imploringly, they looked at us. "Please," they seemed to say, "don't do something crazy."

But we were private citizens now. We could raise all the hell that other groups had raised when we were wearing the shields. There was pushing and jostling. With no one in City

Hall even to listen, frustration mounted and the mood turned uglier. One or two sanitation men took swipes at uniformed cops and were arrested. Then someone started throwing garbage.

A couple of police captains and deputy inspectors appeared with bullhorns. They tried to calm us. They urged us not to bring any more disgrace on the department.

"The department's already disgraced!" someone shouted. A huge cheer rose from the crowd.

"They don't want to know us! They don't want to hear us!" yelled one of the leaders of the demonstration. "Well, we'll make them know us! We'll make them hear us!"

Another roar went up. The tension on both sides of the police line was brittle enough to break.

"Let's take the Brooklyn Bridge!" someone yelled. I was right with them as the entire milling, surging crowd turned and marched toward the bridge. The demonstration leaders, bearing large American flags, forged to the front. Then a mounted division moved to intercept them. I expected war to begin right there. But it didn't.

One of the uniformed officers on horseback leaned down to a leader of the crowd, his former partner. "Follow us!" he said. And led by the mounted division, we marched to the bridge. There the demonstration slipped further out of control as the dismissed cops, fire fighters, and sanitation men spilled into the roadway of the bridge and brought traffic to a halt. Motorists cursed at us. We cursed back. The air was purple with profanities. Traffic backed up into Manhattan, into Brooklyn, and up and down the F.D.R. Drive.

A deputy inspector appeared with a bullhorn. He was as upset as any of us. Many of the men knew him and recognized him as a straightforward guy. When he addressed us his eyes filled with tears. "I know what you guys are going through. It's a disgrace not only to the city but to this department what's been done to you. But, please. I'm begging you. Don't make it worse. You're still professionals. I swear to you that eventually you'll come back if you want to. Please, please! Don't leave the job this way."

Gradually, some of the men moved from the roadway and the crowd began to thin. Like a storm subsiding from its spent fury, so did our demonstration. But none of the anger was gone.

We had caused a massive traffic tie-up that lasted through the rush hour and into the evening. As usual, the citizens and the newspapers saw us as the villains. Cops, they said, had no moral right to behave like that.

By late evening I was back uptown on West Twentieth Street in the middle of the parking lot amid a handful of scattered driverless cars. I was alone. I sat on the front fender of my car, not wanting to go home, not able to return to the precinct.

As I held my face in my hands for several long, soothing seconds, I could see the previous eighteen months spiraling before me with everything right there at once...

The woman lying beneath the bus, one leg amputated, the other mangled...

The doped-out Vietnam veteran on West Seventeenth Street whirling at me and pulling the trigger of his loaded pistol...

Thanksgiving Day, a family dispute: a cluttered tenement apartment, three little girls screaming, an hysterical wife, the dinner table overturned, a window broken, the turkey smashed against the wall, the father barricaded in the bathroom with a carving knife in each fist...

Two gays, resplendent in pastels and drunk out of their

minds at 3 A.M. on a Sunday morning, approaching our parked car with a request to be handcuffed and beaten up. "We like it!" they chirp in unison...

At Madison Square Garden during a rally for the Reverend Sun Myung Moon, the Korean evangelist, an anti-Moon crowd grows outside. Someone shoves the wooden horses that form the police barricade. My hand is caught between two slabs of wood and five bones are broken. Yet I stay on duty because there are no reinforcements and a riot is easier to stop before it starts...

On foot patrol at 2 A.M. on a sultry night in July, I find a frightened four-year-old girl wandering Tenth Avenue. I coax her to describe the block where she lives and I take her hand and walk her home.

Her mother is sitting out on the stoop, sipping beer from a quart bottle.

She sees us coming and explodes with anger.

"What you hasslin' my kid for?" the mother screams, reaching forward and jerking the child's hand away from mine. "Goddamned fuckin' cops! Always hasslin' babies!"

I have stopped a doctor for driving sixty-five miles an hour across a crowded Fourteenth Street. When I inquire how fast he thought he was going, he becomes abusive. He tells me he is an important man and has a right to be in a hurry. Why am I stopping him, he yells, when there are serious criminals at large? I was going to let him off with a warning. Instead, I write him a summons. Now he promises to call my commander and have my job taken away. He demands to know my name and shield number. I give it to him a second time, this time at the bottom of a summons for failure to display a state inspection sticker on his windshield...

My partner and I arrest a punk who has broken the arm of

an eighty-year-old woman on West Twenty-first Street during a robbery that netted eight dollars and fifty-seven cents. How do I tell the woman's family that I have now arrested the same young hoodlum five times—twice armed with a cheap revolver—for similar assaults and other officers in my precinct have busted him nine times. The boy will be home that night. The victim will be in the hospital a month, will lose partial mobility of her arm and was lucky she wasn't killed. The boy is fourteen and family court keeps releasing him. When he eventually kills someone, Family Court will probably release him again . . .

The visions merge. It is all one ceaseless shift, from midnight to eight to four to midnight, over and over again. Everything is happening at once. The job is out there begging to be done. And the city won't let me do it.

As I open my eyes, the evening is darker and the streetlights seem brighter. I am still alone in the parking lot—a civilian, just like millions of other New Yorkers. I have no shield and no weapon, only a termination paper stuffed into my wallet.

Maybe we should have torn down the bridge, I think angrily. Maybe we should have forced our brother officers to arrest us. But no, I decide. That isn't the way, either. All my life I have been opposed to tearing things down just to make a point. Enraged and frustrated as I am, I cannot start now.

When I arrived home there were various messages for me. Mother had taken the calls while I was out. As I looked through them, one in particular caught my eye.

"What's this?" I asked.

"A Mr. Caproni," she said, looking over my shoulder. "He said you know him."

Caproni. Caproni. I turned the name over. Then I remembered the two F.B.I. agents who had come to the precinct several months earlier.

"If it's important he'll call back," I said.

"That's what he said," she replied.

I looked up. "What?"

"He said it was important. And that he'd call back."

About ten days later, half the men who'd been laid off were given their jobs back. A typical political stunt: take away a lot, give back a little, and pretend you're a hero. Jimmy, Roddy, and my brother-in-law Mike went back on the job, thanks to seniority. I and twenty-five hundred others remained off the force.

When I grew up, a man who lost his job went out and found another. If it wasn't exactly what he wanted to do, that was unfortunate. But unemployment and welfare we regarded as the bottom of the barrel. No one owes anyone a living.

I did some odd jobs with other cops at first—a bit of carpentry and housepainting, a little plumbing, and a fair amount of electrical work. Then I was offered the position of security director at Majors Department Store in Staten Island. The job offered me something resembling police work—if chasing shoplifters all day can be considered police work—and allowed me to get my pistol permit back. So I took it.

Meanwhile, Caproni and Daley had their plans for me, too. There is little that I can say about my undercover work for the F.B.I. I had no gun and no shield, but technically I was still on the payroll of the New York City Police Department as well as the F.B.I. No one in the NYPD below the rank of Inspector, however, had access to where I was or what I was doing.

I collected my pay in an unusual manner.

Every other Thursday evening I would venture into Manhattan and mingle with the theater crowds around Times Square. After making sure that no one was shadowing me, I would go to a hot dog vendor directly under the huge Coca-Cola sign and buy a hot dog. I would be given two napkins. One napkin was to keep the mustard off my fingers. The other contained my pay in cash. I was to say nothing to the vendor, but if I was in any sort of trouble or wished to arrange a meeting with Caproni or Daley, the signal was to be a newspaper folded under my left arm. The vendor, too, was an undercover officer.

Somewhere along the line, my identity came under suspicion to those I was working against. First the tires of my car were slashed. Then the windows of my house were smashed in with bricks.

If I quit my undercover work, I felt at that time, I would be admitting to what I'd been doing. Plus I can be stubborn. So I stayed in place.

A month after I'd bought four new tires for my car and installed new glass in my home, I went out to my car one morning and noticed that the rear windshield had four large bulletholes in it. And still I didn't take the hint.

A short time later, as I was driving home on the Brooklyn-Queens Expressway, the front tire flew cleanly off my car. I spun wildly at sixty miles an hour, careened through traffic, up against a concrete and steel divider, and across a safety island.

Miraculously, no one was hurt. But this time, I took the hint. On my next trip to buy a hot dog, I carried a thick folded newspaper under my left arm.

I met Special Agent Caproni for a final time in Bryant Park behind the Public Library. I told him I wanted out. He asked me if I was sure. I told him I was damned sure.

"The information you've been getting for us," Caproni said, "is eventually going to put people in jail." He drew on a cigarette as he scanned Bryant Park. He spoke without looking at me. "Do you still carry your thirty-eight?"

"I don't have an off-duty permit anymore," I answered.

"Better carry it anyway," he mused. "Better to be judged by twelve men than carried out of church by six." Then he paused and did look at me. "Better make it a permanent part of your clothes," he said. "These guys have long memories."

By a strange coincidence, I was rehired onto the New York City Police Department about ten days later. I returned to my old job in the Tenth Precinct. Then, magically, someone acted on one of my earlier transfer forms and I was re-assigned to the Sixty-eighth Precinct in Brooklyn—Bay Ridge, my old neighborhood—where I worked for two years as a patrolman among the people, churches, bars, and schools that I had known as a boy.

I also became engaged again to a girl named Kathlene. Foolishly, we had very few serious conversations until after we'd set a marriage date. I had particular ideas; so did she. Once again, the ring was returned.

I used the money to buy a fire engine, strange as it sounds, because a small group of friends and I were disturbed that the kids we knew had no way to acquaint themselves with police or fire work until it was actually time to make a career choice. So we all chipped in and bought a retired 1954 fire engine from the city. Then we organized the Explorers Post for teenagers who wanted to learn the techniques of fire fighting.

About this time, when I was working in the Six-eight, I decided that I wanted to do a particular type of police work, the sort that differs every day, is somewhat more exciting, and tends to be the most critical and urgent work a cop can do.

So I applied for Emergency Services.

I was accepted in February 1980.

Nine

MICHAEL

ONE thing Michael remembers about juvenile court in Memphis is the chair. He was made to sit in it for hours until his case was called. Before that he'd been given a pair of blue jeans that were too big, a sweat shirt that was too small, and sneakers that had been worn by somebody else.

Then there was the bus. The bus with the dirty windows with the wire over them and the driver who doesn't talk while he drives the kids to Hina Street for rehabilitation.

After a week, the juvenile court put Michael on the bus for Hina Street with a bunch of young muggers and car thieves and kids who used and sold dope. It was said of one black kid who didn't ever talk that he'd stabbed someone. The kid looked about twelve.

Michael stayed at Hina Street for a few months. He didn't get along. He got in fights with the kids. He got in fights with the staff. He was put in a straight jacket and then in seclusion. Finally he was sent to the Spencer Youth Center in Nashville.

Michael remembers the long lines for the awful meals, and the cells. There were also boxing matches in the evening. If somebody called your name, you had to go out and box with him. The big kids often called Michael's name.

That same year a minister by the name of Bergeron visited Spencer Youth. Mr. Bergeron took an interest in Michael. He thought Michael was in over his head. He had seen similar situations in the past and in such cases, the institution only made things worse. So he spent some time talking to Michael. Many hours over many days, in fact. He asked Michael if he'd like to try living in a house with a family again.

"Yes, sir. I would," Michael said.

"I can get you released from here on a technicality," Mr. Bergeron told him. "You can move into my house. For a short time, at least. I have two other sons."

"I'd like that," Michael said.

On St. Patrick's Day Michael moved in with the Bergerons. The two sons were much older, nineteen and twenty. Though Mrs. Bergeron was very kind, it was not easy for Michael because everyone was a stranger. But the family got Michael back in school and he did well.

Summer came. The neighborhood youngsters liked to party. There was a lot of beer and hard liquor around and plenty of grass if you could get a few dollars together. Mr. Bergeron warned Michael about the beer and the grass.

That August Michael met Darlene, a lovely girl from Chicago who was visiting relatives in Tennessee. She had dark hair and long tan legs. She was sixteen and more experienced about some things than Michael.

Before Labor Day, Darlene went back to Chicago. But she

was still in Michael's thoughts. Michael asked Mr. Bergeron if he could visit her.

"By yourself?" Mr. Bergeron asked.

"Yes, sir. I can get to Chicago by myself."

"No, Michael, I'm sorry."

A few days later, Michael ran away to Nashville, where for two weeks he worked in a bar that featured live music, setting up for a blue grass band, waiting on tables, and washing dishes.

Shortly thereafter he hitched a ride to Asheville, North Carolina. Then he continued eastward to Morgantown, where a family of fundamentalists took him in.

Early one morning, Michael took the family car keys off the kitchen table. He did not have a driver's license but he knew all about cars. Slipping behind the wheel, he stepped on the accelerator and was gone.

Michael drove westward through North Carolina and into Tennessee. He drove the entire width of the state, not knowing exactly where he was going. Then, almost out of gas and with very little money, he saw a familiar sign. He was near Somerville, site of the John S. Wilder Development Center, his first correctional institution. He left the road, intent on dropping in on his old friends.

When Michael entered the day room, he saw several familiar faces. He sat with the boys, smoking and laughing, and telling tales. "I got my car," he boasted, motioning to the vehicle in the parking lot, "and I graduated from high school already. I'm doing just great."

It was all pretty good fun until a man who happened to be teaching at Wilder that afternoon heard the ruckus. James Forrest then stepped into the day room and saw the boy who'd fled his home sixteen months before.

"Hey, Michael," Forrest said, extending his hand. "How are you?"

Michael was surprised to see his one-time foster father and further surprised by his cordiality. "Oh. Hello, sir," he said. "I'm doing fine."

"Where are you living?" Forrest asked.

"Oh, I have a job lined up in Chicago," Michael began. "I'm just driving through. Thought I'd stop by and say hello."

"That's very thoughtful of you," said the teacher. "Which car is yours?"

Mike proudly pointed out the vehicle in the parking lot. Jim Forrest chatted for a few more minutes, then departed. Michael sat down again and gave a pained smile to his friends as the boys enjoyed a good laugh at how easily one of their teachers had been duped.

Moments later Wilder's headmaster was at the window of his office, his telephone raised to his ear. Forrest stood nearby as the headmaster read the license plate number of Michael's car to the North Carolina State Police.

Returning to the day room, Jim Forrest walked toward Michael. He held out his hand. "The car keys," he said.

"The what, sir?"

Forrest spoke calmly, "Don't make it any worse, Michael. I know the car is stolen."

Michael froze. From the status of hero in the eyes of his friends, he had plummeted to that of perfect fool—sitting inside a correctional institution with the state police on the way.

Forrest's hand was extended, his palm open. Michael reached slowly into his pocket and handed over the car keys. Michael's friends exploded with laughter.

Michael had taken the car from North Carolina six days after his seventeenth birthday, April 4, 1981. Seventeen was legal age in Tennessee and North Carolina. Michael was in trouble. The charge was Grand Larceny–Auto. The funda-mentalist family in Morgantown felt betrayed. They not only wanted their car back but were pressing charges. Extradited by North Carolina, he was returned to Asheville's county jail in handcuffs.

Michael shared a cell with two other seventeen-year-olds. One had robbed a gas station. The other was a shoplifter. Neither said much. Michael's case wasn't scheduled for a week and a half.

Jail gave him time to think. He had a lot of questions, but few answers. He wished he had gone to Chicago to find Dar-lene. Maybe they could have gotten married and lived happily ever after. But how does anyone live happily ever after, he wondered.

Michael fashioned a mixture of Coca-Cola, coffee, cigarette ashes, and water in a paper cup. Then, using an old jail house method, he began to tattoo his left wrist, using a sharpened pencil and the point of a safety pin.

The D took a day and the skin smarted and was sore. The A was perfectly symmetrical. The R and the L hardly hurt at all. By the time DARLENE read in block black letters across his wrist, it just itched a little.

A legal aid lawyer kept coming to see Michael, a young man in his twenties named Richard. He took Michael to court one day and soon began talking about how Michael Buchanan was a first-time offender and the court should find some so-lution other than prison. But juvenile detention centers were out; Michael was too old. Foster homes were no longer a consideration. And the State of Tennessee refused to take him back: the boy was of legal age with a felony record.

Richard decided to play his trump card. The court would agree to release Michael if Michael would enlist in the United

States Army. The army, everyone felt, would do him good.

Reluctantly, Michael agreed. Richard drew up the proper papers. And after thirty-one days in jail, Michael was released in the temporary custody of a local church.

But as enlistment day drew near, Michael began to have misgivings. Midway between the parsonage and the lawyer's office was a bus terminal. One of the transport companies had a special weekend fare to Cleveland or to Cincinnati. Michael decided against the army.

Ten

THERE is a bulletin board in the front vestibule of the precinct house, just a few feet from the plaque memorializing Pat O'Connor. Whenever men from our outfit reach the papers, the clipping goes up there. It's June 1981 and as I enter the precinct I see the pictures of my two friends, Gary Gorman and Al Sheppard.

The day before, working together on a shift, they had rescued a man from the Hudson River. A photographer from the *Daily News* was present and today Gary and Shep are in the centerfold. The rescue was what we call "good police work." A life was saved because officers were on the scene and did their job.

But as I enter the locker room and pull up a chair at the Gray Table, no one is talking about the rescue. Everyone is watching the television above the coffee maker at the rear of the room.

I sit down next to Sheppard, who is chain smoking as usual and twitching his blond moustache. His focus is glued on the screen. I look up and I blink. Paul Newman in the uniform of a New York City police officer is chasing minority stereotype across a vacant lot.

"What's this?" I asked.

"*Ft. Apache, The Bronx*," Shep answers, a smile creeping across his face. "Do you believe it? Paul Newman as a street cop in the Four-four."

There are hoots from the older guys behind me as a silver-haired Paul Newman gains on his suspect. "Go get him, Paul!" someone yells.

"Don't get your uniform dirty!" someone else yells.

"Hey!" Sheppard suddenly blurts out. "Look at that! Paul Newman is wearing white socks!"

Now there are peals of laughter from around the Gray Table. White socks with a uniform would cost an officer a command discipline. Collect enough command disciplines and you'll start seeing a dent in your paycheck. Paul Newman tackles his perpetrator and does not get a command discipline.

"This movie's full of shit," says Tommy McCarthy. "Ten minutes ago they had these Emergency Service guys on the roof preparing to break into an apartment to end a hostage situation. So what do they do? They lower Paul Newman down the side of the building and let this dumb-assed precinct cop do the job."

"Paul Newman is the star," Gary answers. "He's got to break in."

"E Men aren't stars," Shep adds. "Except for Richie Seaberg and Captain Hanratty."

Everyone grins because Richie Seaberg, perhaps the most dedicated man in our unit, and Captain Hanratty, our commander, have just appeared. Their heads bolt in our direction as they hear their names mentioned.

I look back to the television and chuckle. As usual, Hollywood has taken an inaccurate view of how cops live and work. Precinct cops like Paul Newman do not wear white socks. Street guys like *Starsky and Hutch* do not fire warning shots across rooftops. No lieutenant, such as Kojak, goes out and cracks cases. Lieutenants sit at desks and administer. I suppose if anything comes close to the mark, it's *Police Story* and *Hill Street Blues*. I like *Quincy*. It's entertaining and at least it's not *in*accurate.

Attention lags from the movie. Sheppard turns to Paul Redecha, his usual partner, and complains about the way the Fire Department is assuming more and more of the police rescue procedures. Shep worries about our unit being disbanded with the Fire Department taking over all rescue work in the city.

Redecha only smiles. Paulie is referred to in the precinct as the Giant or The Gentle Giant. He is six feet five. A native New Yorker who grew up in Yorkville, Paulie once got tired of listening to Sheppard complain about the fire department. So he picked up his five-foot-ten partner, and dropped him head first into the precinct trash barrel.

"No friggin' fire department is going to take over Emergency work, Sheppard," Tommy McCarthy sourly informs him. "Who's going to rescue the Rubber Men when they get stuck in elevators?"

The comment brings laughter from the room. More than once recently, Emergency had had to unlock elevators for trapped smoke-eaters. No one knows why the firemen aren't getting elevator training. But apparently they aren't.

Sgt. Andy Stewart, one of the best in our division, casually mentions that he has applied for a transfer to Harbor Patrol. We protest and tell him that if his transfer is approved, we will hold him hostage until Harbor offers us free cruises around Manhattan in the summer.

"Can you swim, Sarge?" Gary asks, maintaining a straight face.

"No," Sgt. Stewart answers, equally straight. The sergeant can swim like a fish.

"Gary likes to swim, don't you, Gary?" Shep says, pushing Gary's cap over his face. Gary has been in the water a lot lately. A week before the Hudson River rescue, he and I took a call for two men who'd been seen in the water under the Queensboro Bridge. As soon as we confirmed the call, we hit the siren in the R.E.P. and took off for the United Nations, about a mile down the East River from the Queensboro. I held the rope as Gary swam out to the middle where two bodies seemed to be clinging to each other.

One body was a certified floater, a wino who'd been dead for days. The other was a very frightened Spanish-speaking teenager who'd seen the floater and dived in, thinking he was saving a life. Exhausted by the time he reached the dead body, he clung to it until Gary brought him in.

"There's nothing I like more than a swim," Gary agrees with a shudder.

Sgt. Stewart reappears with the orders of the day. "Okay, men, time to work!" he calls out.

A few minutes past midnight, we return to our precinct. The clipping of Shep and Gary has been torn into small confetti-sized pieces and scattered onto the floor. It is our reminder that a generation gap still exists on the force and within our squad. Too bad, because we are stuck with each other.

The summer is a hectic time for police and there is no indication that this summer will be any different.

Later in the season, in August, I have my two-week vacation. I will travel upstate to Ellenville in the Catskill Mountains. There I own two campers that I share with my family. This summer my mother and sister will accompany me. Eileen's husband, Mike O'Connell, will try to get off from the Senior Citizens' Anti-crime Unit for those same weeks. Their three children will be with us together with as many scouts from the Explorers' Post as I can afford to take. We will camp out and hike through the woods and listen to birds under clear summer skies. The nights will be quiet. No stabbings, no armed robberies, no bodies pinned inside wrecked automobiles.

But my vacation is still weeks away on the other side of the hottest days of the year.

At 2:30 A.M. I am home but I cannot sleep. I am haunted this evening by a three-year-old incident that happened in West Harlem. I wasn't even there. Friends of mine were.

Gary and Shep were working together in one of the R.E.P.'s assigned to upper Manhattan. They received a call for a ten ten, an unidentified man with a gun.

They responded to a block on West One-hundred-thirty-eighth where a man with a police record named Luther Jones had fired shots at his mother. Witnesses directed Gary and Shep to a nearby tenement.

They called for a back-up. Jones was said to be armed with a long weapon, either a rifle or a shotgun. Gary and Shep put on their flak jackets, withdrew shotguns from the R.E.P. and entered the building.

They walked up two rickety flights of stairs, stepping over food containers, broken bottles, and discarded needles. The building was abandoned, but showed signs of activity from day to day.

Now, of course, there was no sound, other than the two

police officers, Gary about thirty feet in front of Shep, slowly climbing the creaking, poorly lit stairs.

On the third floor Gary faced an open door that led into a kitchen. He heard movement within the apartment. His weapon ready, he signaled Shep he was going in. Quietly, alertly, Shep followed.

Gary passed through the kitchen and along a dark hallway with crumbling plaster. He continued to hear movement somewhere, but he pressed on. At the next doorway, he surprised a man holding a pistol. The man matched the description of the suspect.

Gary swung his weapon toward the man. "Police officer! Freeze!" he blurted.

The man jumped, but did not turn. He dropped his weapon. The suspect said nothing.

"Get your hands up and get against the wall!"

The suspect obeyed. He moved slowly, but moved as ordered.

Gary stepped carefully into the room, never taking his eyes off his prisoner. He stepped past two large discarded mattresses that lay in the center of the floor and eased his way through a clutter of bottles and cans.

To Gary's left was a large refrigerator, one of the few furnishings in the room. Gary paid no attention to it.

Then out of the corner of his eye—for an agonizing split second that will be vivid in Gary's mind forever—he saw a movement and realized his mistake.

There were two men in the room besides Gary. And the figure in the corner of Gary's view held a shotgun shouldered and aimed to fire. Gary had let a gunman get the drop on him.

"Gary!" It was Shep's voice. Gary whirled toward the man preparing to shoot him. But before Gary could squeeze the trigger of his own weapon, the room exploded with a deafening, murderous blast.

By all odds, Gary should have been dead.

Except the roar that filled the room was from Sheppard's gun. And that was it.

Gary and Shep stared at each other and at what had happened. Until this moment, neither had ever fired a heavy weapon in the line of duty. Now a human being lay dead. Any cop will tell you that no matter what the situation, no matter how clear the self-defense, no matter how right you were in pulling the trigger, when you take a life, it stays with you forever. Because you have failed to resolve the situation peacefully, it haunts you. You did what had to be done, but a human life has been lost.

"And you know the eerie part?" Gary asked me when I first learned of the incident. "One week later, Shep and I had another call a few blocks away in the same neighborhood. We went up a similar flight of stairs down a hallway and into the same sort of apartment. We're both carrying shotguns again. Suddenly, I say to Shep, 'There he is! There he is!' and I aim the shotgun, tighten my finger on the trigger, and am just about to fire. 'Where? Where?' Shep is saying. Then I realize that I'm looking at a broomstick leaning out of a curtained closet."

Just as I feared, the city is getting meaner as the thermometer nears ninety.

A domestic quarrel turns into a multiple stabbing. Half a family dies. The cries of an uncomfortable infant in a sweltering slum apartment trigger a case of child abuse: a two-month-old scalded in a bathtub. But the court returns the child to her parents. Two automobiles converge on the same parking place at the same time and a dispute over thirteen feet of curb space turns into one dead and one under arrest for second-degree murder.

Two lifelong buddies are drinking with each other at a bar in Hell's Kitchen. It is three o'clock on a scorching afternoon. The air conditioning is not working and the two men argue whether Carmen Basilio knocked out Sugar Ray Robinson once or twice in the mid-1950s.

"You wait here," one man says. "I'm going to look it up."

He returns with a .45 caliber souvenir from World War II and calmly shoots his lifelong friend through the head. Then he drops the pistol on the barroom floor and settles back down.

"It sure is hot in here," he says to the bartender as he waits for the police.

Our R.E.P. is not yet air conditioned and we soak through our uniforms even on an evening shift. "It sure is hot in here," I find myself saying to Gary. We are barely past the Fourth of July.

At a restaurant in Chinatown we are looking at the bodies of two men—both young and Chinese. One is slumped over a table. The meal he never got to finish is caked with blood, and the chop sticks he used are still clutched tightly in his fist. The other young man is sprawled across the floor, his right arm fully extended, the other folded across his bullet-punctured chest. Plate glass walls at street level allow more than a hundred evening strollers to observe the carnage.

Part of our training in Emergency Services is the recovery of spent rounds of ammunition. That is why Gary and I are here along with four uniformed cops from the Fifth Precinct and two homicide detectives from a Manhattan South Homicide Task Force. Somewhere in this restaurant are seven spent rounds.

A liaison man from the neighborhood, a Chinese-American

who was born in Canton during the time of Chiang Kai-shek, tells us that the two dead boys were from Peking and were members of a very bad gang.

"Did anyone see who shot them?" asks a detective. "How many gunmen were there?"

The man from Canton reflects on the City of Peking and what a terrible place it is.

"These guys have enemies," I say to him. "Who were they?"

"Very bad gang, also," he answers with a mild grin. "Very worse very bad gang."

The detective turns to me. "The place was packed. Maybe a hundred people. And nobody saw anything."

The place is not packed now and the management is anxious to get the bodies out so they can mop up and get their customers back in. Gary and I dig two bullets out of the plaster wall. We find three more on the floor. Two other bullets remain in each body. The temperature is ninety degrees. Since the customers have left, the management has turned off the air conditioning.

The two detectives look spectacularly disinterested. They have seven other unsolved gang slayings of young men in Chinatown. They lounge at one of the tables as Gary and I finish.

"You don't know how lucky these two guys were," one of the detectives can't resist saying.

"Why?" Gary asks.

"We had another stiff last week. Found him in the basement of a movie theater on East Broadway. They cut his dick off and stuffed it in his mouth. Then they shot his eyes out."

"Nice," I answer.

The detective shrugs and looks around to see if there is anything cold to drink.

"Very bad gang," says the old man, nodding again. There

are twenty-three thousand police officers in New York City. Two of them speak Chinese. Perhaps this is part of our problem.

"The worst execution I ever saw," Gary muses as we ride back uptown, "was Carmine Galante. Remember, Billy? He got whacked out in the rear of a restaurant in Brooklyn. I think they put a dozen bullets in him or through him. When he lay on the floor dead, his cigar was clenched in his teeth. It was still smoking when we arrived."

Gary was with Emergency back in the summer of 1979 when Galante, the reputed head of the Mafia in the United States, was shot during an otherwise uneventful spaghetti lunch. Gary and his partner, Mike Morgan, were called in to recover the spent rounds.

"We had been in the restaurant for about ten minutes," Gary continues as we merge with the traffic on Houston Street, "when this captain from Brooklyn Homicide appears. He starts walking around, looking at everything, examining everything. 'I can't believe it,' he says over and over. 'I can't believe it.' So finally I ask, 'What's the matter, Cap?' He looks at me with a perfectly straight face. 'I'm retiring today,' he says, 'and so is Carmine.'"

A week later, we are called to an expensive residential building on West Fifty-seventh Street. A very shaken maintenance man is waiting for us behind the building. Two precinct cops are with him.

"What's the problem?" I ask as Gary and I arrive.

One of the cops motions with his head toward a trash compactor. "See for yourself," he says.

We walk to a pile of garbage that was in the process of being compacted. Staring up at us from among the coffee grounds, smashed cereal boxes, and stained old newspapers, is a human head.

The maintenance man then summons all his courage and tells us what he has not yet told the precinct cops.

"Four D," he says. That is the apartment of the man whose head is in the garbage bin.

Sheppard and Redecha, responding to the same call, now join us. At Apartment 4-D, a small frail woman answers our knock.

"Yes?" she says, seeing four large police officers in front of her. Already Gary and I notice the scent we know so well. "Have you come to see me?" she asks. "My husband doesn't live here anymore."

There is really no mystery. The woman's husband, we have already learned from the doormen, took care of his wife for many years so that she could live at home and not be institutionalized. About two weeks ago, at the breakfast table, he had evidently slumped over and died. She did not know what to do. So she didn't do anything.

The rest of his body is still there. A day or so earlier she had tried to move it. The flesh had decomposed and the head came off. She did what was to her the logical thing. She wrapped it in newspaper and tried to dispose of it.

Shep and Paulie sit with the woman in the living room, speaking to her gently until an ambulance can arrive. Gary and I remain in the kitchen. The apartment, of course, reflects the woman's compromised mental state. There is no food anywhere, for example, other than a full carton of ice cream on the kitchen table. It appears to have been there for many days.

Gary and I go for a body bag, the Scott Air Packs, and rubber gloves.

When we return, the woman tells Shep that he is a nice young man and if he says we are here to help her, she will trust him. Her wrinkled hands tremble slightly as she wrings a cloth handkerchief. I glance around the apartment. Once, about forty years ago, this must have been at the peak of fashion. But little appears to have changed since D-Day.

An ambulance attendant arrives. He deals patiently with the woman. Shep asks if he can help her downstairs. No, she tells him, she will go with the attendant if she can just be allowed to get her coat.

"Sure," Shep says.

She goes to a closet and gets her fur, a square-shouldered chubby from another era.

"Goodbye, officers," she says. Then she walks slowly past us out into the summer heat. There are tears welling in her eyes. She is crying. I feel myself taking a bite on my lower lip as I watch her go.

Somedays, I feel like putting my hands over my face and crying. Or I feel like going to some isolated room and screaming, "Enough!"

But then the moment passes. Shep, Paulie, Gary, and I kick it around between us or thrash it out with the other men at the Gray Table. Yet when we take off the uniforms and walk out the precinct door, we cannot allow it to go home with us. The day we start bringing our job home is the day we should quit as cops. Or so we have been told.

I am seeing a girl named Tina about once a week. She belongs to my church, which is where we met. She is several years younger than I and has a good job in Manhattan. She probably earns more than I do. Times change.

I like Tina very much. But I am not in love. I would hesitate to call her my girlfriend. Recently, she has been asking me tactful questions about my two engagements and why they were broken off.

I answer honestly but not fully. I know she is thinking about her future, just as I have been thinking about mine.

Mother likes Tina and would be tickled pink to welcome a third daughter-in-law into the family. But I feel ill prepared to make such a sacred personal commitment. My life feels strangely unsettled, perhaps reflecting the craziness of the city that surrounds me.

Inspired by some hallucinogenic drug, a young woman jumps out of a third-floor window and is impaled on the spikes of an iron fence. But she is alive. So is the six-month fetus she carries within her. Ten Emergency cops work with acetylene torches to free her from the spikes. She is taken to Bellevue and, incredibly, lives. Even her pregnancy survives.

A boy in a warehouse is riding on top of a freight elevator, a popular game in some sections of the city. He is looking down, five, six, seven, eight flights, watching as the car he rides rises from the basement. He forgets that the space through which he is staring down is the space through which the elevator's one-ton counterbalance descends.

Richie Seaberg, "Chips" Lasalle, Gary, and I are called to an address in the West Thirties where a man has been spotted on the roof with a machine gun. We get the heavy weapons out of the truck, put on our flak jackets, and trace the man to his apartment. Gary and Chips cover his front door. Richie Seaberg and I climb the fire escape to arrive at the man's rear window.

We can see in. He has dozens of guns in the apartment. Pistols. Rifles. Submachine guns. A mortar launcher. The man is prepared for the next world war and walks around with two weapons in his hands.

I aim my shotgun at him. So does Richie. At a pre-arranged moment, Chips and Gary knock on the front door and from the rear window I scream an order for the man to freeze. My finger is tensed on the trigger of my shotgun. The man stares at us. Then he drops his weapons.

Inside the apartment, we discover that every single piece of his arsenal is plastic.

After the shift is finished, I sit in the R.E.P. by myself for several long moments. I think back to my finger tightening on the trigger of the shotgun.

I can imagine the roar of my weapon and I can visualize the man being blown apart by my shot. God have mercy on me. I came within a quarter inch of killing an unarmed man.

But how was I to know? How will I know the next time?

July steams. August broils. The summer is one bomb, one D.O.A., one severed limb, one floater, one stabbing, one battered child, one hostage, one horror after another. It simply won't stop.

More than anything else in the world, I would like to know that my job means something. I would like to know that we are reaching people, that we are helping them. But there is only more of the August heat and more human misery.

I finish an evening shift, I unwind for a few minutes at the precinct, and I go home. I will sleep for five hours, then, because of manpower shortages and scheduling irregularities, I will return the same morning to work an 8 A.M. shift. At that time, the day—and what I do for a living—will start all over again.

MICHAEL

It is eight in the evening. Michael is scrubbing dinner plates in the steel sink filled with steaming water. He works in the rear of Simone's, a small family restaurant in Cincinnati. Michael's companions in the kitchen scrub area are the chattering busboys who barge past him, dump piles of plates and glasses onto the adjoining wash counter and then leave. There is also a television.

He is watching *The Waltons,* deeply intrigued by the bonds within a rural American family of the 1930s. Families interest Michael. The program breaks for a commercial. People Express, a small, aggressively marketed eastern airline, offers a special fare to New York. Thirty-five dollars one way.

Michael lives at Simone's on an old mattress in the back room. Not great. But it is secure and safe. He has a roof as well as food. And there is the television.

A few nights later, *King Kong* is on. King Kong picks up a beautiful girl, Jessica Lange, in the palm of his hand and scales the World Trade Center in New York City. New York seems exciting; and the vision remains with Michael. He thinks about Jessica Lange, those tall buildings, those screaming sirens and all that excitement for several days.

One evening a few weeks later, Michael is setting up tables in the restaurant's dining area. The kitchen has closed. It is very late. A young couple are still lingering over their beer. The man and woman are just back from a weekend in New York.

As Michael sets up a neighboring table, he falls into conversation with them.

"A fabulous place," the man says. "New York. Big. Clean. Exciting. And the people. Don't let anybody kid you. The people are friendly."

"I saw *King Kong,*" Michael volunteers, only half facetiously. "Is that what New York is like?"

The man points an index finger at him. "That's exactly what New York is like," he says. "Always something big going on. Not like Norwood, Ohio." The man drains his beer. "And all the women," he concludes, "all the women look like Jessica Lange." His wife throws him a sour glare. "Except my wife," the man adds quickly. "My wife is more beautiful than Jessica Lange."

"What about jobs?" Michael asks. "Are there jobs in New York?"

"Thousands of them. Just for the asking. Good jobs." The man looks curiously at Michael "What kind of job do you want?"

Michael is slightly embarrassed. "Something better than this."

"You finish high school yet?"

"Yes," Michael lies.

"Then you can get any job you want in New York."

"Don't tell him that," the woman interjects peevishly. "You'll get his hopes up."

The man clumsily wraps his arm around his wife's shoulders as they stand. "My wife has had too much to drink," he announces with labored clarity. "I better take her home. She has my hopes up now. My hopes and everything else."

Michael gives them a sheepish smile.

"Brute!" the woman teases her husband. But she allows him to give her a long kiss on the lips. The couple place twenty dollars on the table to settle their bill and leave.

An hour later, Michael is in the back room of the restaurant on his mattress. He watches the late movie on the only station that the battered black and white television still receives. The movie breaks for a commercial.

Again, People Express. Thirty-five dollars from Greater

Cincinnati Airport to Newark. Only thirty-five dollars to the bright lights and fast avenues of New York City.

Hell, Michael figures, that's not so much.

Eleven

AT the Gray Table a week later, we are talking numbers. The strength of the Emergency Service squads around the five boroughs has dropped to one hundred eighty-four men and one woman. The department maintains that our ideal manpower is three hundred. So we are at two-thirds effectiveness unless every member realizes that he or she must do a job and a half each day.

Worse, some of the best men in our squad are contemplating leaving. John Lannigan has been on the job for so long that his son is going to join him within a few months. Same for Georgie Toth. Mike McCrory, a true veteran, will retire next August. Jimmy Hatcher wants to go to the Bomb Squad. Richie Mueller wants to transfer to the Nine Truck, which is Emergency in Brooklyn.

Captan Hanratty tells us that we'll be getting new men in the unit in January, when each of us will work with a new man and train him, see if he can do this job. See if he *wants* to do this job. But that is January. This is August.

Today, we are also talking numbers in a different sense. Not just manpower but statistics. The department has released a new set of figures concerning violent crime for the previous four months in Manhattan. Shep has torn the report out of the New York *Post* and left it in the center of the table.

"You know what I think?" Tom McCarthy asks, glancing at the headline. "I think the department plays around with those figures to keep them as low as possible. Ever notice how they always drop when the mayor's up for re-election? Imagine the public reaction when the murder total in this city hits two thousand." McCarthy looks around to see who is listening. No one is. So he gets himself some coffee. "Gonna hit two thousand one of these years soon," he says. "And that's the personal opinion of Police Officer Tom McCarthy."

My brother is still working nights in the Seven-two Precinct and I worry about him. Statistics tell us that men working rotating shifts, meaning most of us, take an average of five years off their lives. But men who work steady nights take eight to ten years off their lives.

It is apparent how the stress of the job ages and weakens the men who are around me. But I see it particularly in my brother. I see it in his face and in his eyes, in the lines on his forehead and the gray around his temples at age forty-two.

Statistics report that a disproportionate number of shootings occur on the 12 to 8 A.M. shift, especially between three and six in the morning. Whether people are more tired, under more pressure, or instinctively inclined toward more violence at that hour, I do not know. I only know what the figures tell me.

I think of my friend Bob Manzione. We went through the academy at the same time and for a few days during the layoffs we worked together as house painters. Bob was a good friend, easygoing, generous, always willing to be helpful, with a ready smile.

One evening in 1977, Bob and his partner were chasing a felony suspect in the Tenth Precinct. Bob caught up with the suspect and began wrestling with him. Bob was a big guy. So was the suspect.

Manzione had the suspect pinned to the sidewalk when his partner caught up with them and began to put cuffs on the prisoner. Just then, Bob felt a tightness in his stomach that he'd never experienced before. The tightness turned into a pain that streaked up and down his left side. He released his grip on the prisoner, who broke free.

Bob's partner started to pursue, but realized that Manzione was in trouble. Bob couldn't get his breath. He was doubled over and couldn't get up. His partner called for emergency medical assistance. In the ambulance a few minutes later, Bob Manzione died of a heart attack.

As one of his best friends, it was my job to break the news to his widow. But what can you say to a woman who has just kissed her husband goodbye as on every other day, then opens the door a few hours later to see his friend, two partners, a police captain, and a chaplain?

What, indeed? You are left with a brave, frightened woman who had a husband that morning, but doesn't have one now. Nothing else can possibly matter.

The mayor, the commissioner and the inspectors were at Bob's funeral, and they each said pretty much what they always say at such occasions. I don't doubt their sincerity. It's just that we've all become numb to the situation. Statistics tell us this will happen six to ten times a year.

Bob Manzione was thirty-seven years old when he died.

*   *   *

It is three-thirty on an August afternoon and time to start our shift. Sgt. Stewart calls us to attention and reads us the orders of the day. Like all precinct cops, we receive special instructions before hitting the streets. It is the duty of the sergeant to alert us to anything that may be happening.

"Anyone around the United Nations should be on the lookout for packages or objects lying about," Sgt. Stewart begins. "Police intelligence has a report of a possible P.L.O. bomb in the area. It's just a rumor, but keep your eyes open."

He pulls a pen out of his pocket and calls us in for a close look. "This is new on the street. It's a pen-gun. Watch."

We crowd around as Sgt. Stewart opens what appears to be a fountain pen and chambers a dummy .22 caliber cartridge into the body of the device. The mechanism for pumping ink clicks down to act as a trigger.

"These things are turning up," he says. "The six house found two last week and the Two-three Precinct got another last night. Stay on your toes." He glances down to read from a piece of paper, then looks back at us. "Also, the welfare checks are in the mailboxes today."

He scans the room. There are muffled groans. On the day the welfare checks arrive there is a five-fold increase of wild drunks and barroom brawls.

"And to top it off," he finishes, "we got a full moon. So watch it out there tonight. Could be a heavy shift."

Gary and I walk from the squad room out into the garage, past the One Truck that waits in its usual place. Tommy McCarthy is right behind me as we climb into the cab of our R.E.P.

"Hey, Fox," McCarthy says, a gleam in his eye. "Didn't you take some religious instruction one time?"

"Yeah," I answer. "What about it?"

"Did you hear about the gay priest?"

"What gay priest?" I ask, taking the bait.

"He couldn't decide whether Jesus was divine or simply outrageous."

Gary splits up and McCarthy, bless him, keeps walking.

The Williamsburg Bridge rises high and dark against the moonlit sky. There is a sector car on the Manhattan side when we arrive. Gary and I jump out of our R.E.P. and look up. We both see the man at once.

"Goddamn," Gary says slowly. "The guy's got to be insane."

I exhale a long slow breath, knowing what the evening now holds in store for us.

"Friggin' full moon," I mutter. "Wouldn't you know?"

Far, far overhead maybe fifteen to twenty stories above the steel-treaded roadway of the bridge, there is a shirtless man doing acrobatics along the suspension cable of the Williamsburg. He runs, he jumps, he leaps. He does somersaults. He seems completely uncaring that, as he runs up and down the cables of the bridge with his hands in the air, sudden death awaits his first false step.

And we can hear him screaming, even with the traffic backing up around us.

There is something about the rarefied air at the peak of New York's bridges that attracts only the most unbalanced of our eight million residents. And because the Police Department regards these people as "disturbed individuals," a danger to both themselves and to passersby, our work includes climbing bridges.

A precinct cop from the five house walks over, alternately

looking up and then back at us. Gary and I are pulling the Morrissey belts out of the truck.

"You guys going up there?" he asks.

"Yup. Want to join us?"

"If you wait ten minutes, maybe he'll slip," he suggests.

"If we wait five minutes," I retort, "maybe his wife and kids will be up there with him."

Gary and I begin climbing the foot-wide suspension cable that rises at the side of the bridge. There is a thin support cable that runs up beside it and acts as a handrail. We hold this carefully as we leave the roadway and begin the long trek up into the night.

As it happens, of the fifty-one bridges in New York City, there is one on which our Morrissey belts, ropes, and clips are useless. And that, of course, is the Williamsburg.

Gary and I are already a hundred feet in the air. The trucks and cars below are growing smaller all the time. The city is beginning to stretch out ominously around us and the East River is just a long, wide ribbon of emptiness that will swallow us if we make one bad step.

The man above us sees us coming. He screams and drums his bare chest. We have moved into range to get a better look at him. He is large and muscular, with a wild mane of shaggy hair. He has torn pants and a sneaker on one foot.

He screams at us again and takes off toward the first of the bridge's two towers.

"Be careful!" I shout at Gary against the wind. "Some of the girders aren't secure!"

By now, the man we are chasing has reached a high stretch of suspension cable. He stops, sits, and straddles it.

"Mio padre!" he yells in Spanish as we draw closer. "Mio father! I'm gonna kill my father!" He stands up and gestures wildly at the moon.

The climb is painful. I have a leg over one girder and a foot on another. We pull ourselves along with our arms.

The man above us watches as we approach to within thirty feet of him.

"My father!" he suddenly screams again in a new tremor of hysteria. *"Mio fucking padre!"*

"Hey, settle down, guy!" Gary yells. "No one's going to hurt you! Your father isn't here!"

We are now within twenty feet of where he continues to straddle the suspension cable. He pulls off his remaining sneaker and throws it far out into the night. Gary and I are close enough to stare eye-to-eye at what we have come to know and dread at the summit of these bridges: the unmistakable glow of the truly crazed or chemically possessed. But tonight there is an additional fear. Those huge rippling muscles across his arms and shoulders! He could handle five of us.

Then suddenly he rises up and takes off. I cannot believe it. He stands majestically aloft the suspension cable, drums his chest again, and begins to *run*. He runs along the cable with the balance of a giant cat, dashing up toward the tower, where he disappears from our view.

"Aw, shit..." I groan.

We crawl up the girders to the tower. Gary is ahead of me. Just a few feet from the tower, we stand on the cable the same way our madman did and walk, arms extended for balance, as if we were crossing a tightrope. We keep one eye on the man on the tower platform who is watching us with great amusement.

But mostly we watch our feet, taking very small steps. I must look down. Any loose rivet or patch of grease could be fatal.

Far below I can see the little dots of humanity on the bridge, the knots of people, the distant twinkling red lights of the police vehicles, and the traffic that is bunching and proceeding slowly as motorists watch our high-wire act. Live entertainment tonight, everybody, and no nets.

I do not have time to be scared but I am terrified anyway. *Oh God, be with me now!* The wind gusts slightly and I see Gary wobble an inch or two. Then my partner is on the tower. And so am I.

Approximately thirty-five stories above the roadway and forty-five stories above the river, we are now face-to-face with our tormentor, a man who looks like The Hulk's stronger older brother. We spread apart, Gary to the left, and I to the right, and approach slowly. We know that the Emergency men on the ground are keeping the area clear. This is a psycho. He may jump at any minute.

He turns. Crossing the platform, he runs toward the suspension cable at the north side of the bridge. Gary and I step tentatively after him as the wind begins to whip past us. But we cannot catch the man.

He jumps from the platform onto the foot-wide steel tubing and runs down it at full speed.

He runs and runs. And we follow.

I go first. I studiously watch my feet as I step down the cable, my arms extended for balance. The man, toying with us, is now forty feet ahead. He leaves the cable and swings like Tarzan through the girders. Again, we follow.

We continue to chase him for another twenty minutes across the skyline. He reaches the second tower of the bridge, on the Queens side, and jumps high in the air, still shrieking in Spanish. We follow him from the tower, taking comfort in the fact that at least two-thirds of the bridge is behind us. I know that several cops will be waiting for him on the Queens side of the bridge when he descends.

He slides down part of the suspension cable, then crawls

through the girders. I am more sure of my footing now, even at this height. I am in front of Gary as we begin to follow our madman downward.

Leaning to move from the cable to a girder, I feel a hard gust of wind.

The bridge is suddenly moving beneath me. I jerk backwards to regain my balance—but I cannot!

"Billy! Careful, Billy!" I hear Gary scream. He reaches for me but I am too far in front of him. My feet go out from under me and I fall hard onto the cable. The ground below seems to invite me as I slide.

Suddenly I realize: I am going to fall off this cable and die. Death is that easy. It takes only a fraction of a second yet it seems like slow motion.

I grab onto the sharp wires wrapped around the cable and desperately hold on. Struggling, I manage to get both arms around the cable as my feet and body dangle forty-five stories above the water.

Then the madman turns and I see that he can get to me before Gary can. It will be easy for him to stomp on my fingers and arms and force me to release my grip. I wonder if he will try it. I wonder if Gary will shoot him first.

Instead, the maniac merrily dances just above me, rambling incoherently in a mixture of English and Spanish, before he leaps to the girders and continues down.

"Hang on, Billy!" Gary calls.

"I'm all right!" I call back. "I'm hanging!"

Gary crawls toward the girders where I am trapped. My arms are weak and I wonder how much longer I can hold on. Gary is approaching with a speed that worries me. He reaches down to my belt and shoulders. My arms are exhausted and I cannot lift myself even slightly. Gary stretches.

Never in my life have I been so thankful for the touch of

125

another human being. With the strength of his own arms, he pulls me up until I can manage to haul myself onto the cable. I nod my head to indicate that although I nearly died, I'm just fine.

We look for our man to find that he is now almost at street level where dozens of precinct cops and two teams of Emergency men are awaiting him. Gary and I collect ourselves to concentrate on our descent. When we are a hundred feet above the roadway, our walkie-talkies crackle.

"You guys OK up there?"

"We're all right," Gary answers.

"We got your psycho," the voice says. "Lt. Reilly and an off-duty guy got him when he landed in Queens."

When we reach the roadway our man, still screaming, is there. He has been handcuffed in front of his chest rather than behind his back, the normal police procedure. I do not have to ask why. His arms, shoulders, and upper chest are so over-developed that he is unable to join his wrists behind his back.

He is our arrest. Gary, Mike Stapleton, Lt. Reilly, and I take him to Bellevue Psychiatric, where we present him to a small, bearded doctor in a white lab coat.

The doctor looks him up and down. "This is my patient?" the psychiatrist asks.

"Yes, sir," Gary says.

"Uncuff him."

The suspect looks at us and grins, his eyes shining.

"Look, doc," I begin, "I think you should know—"

"Uncuff him," the doctor repeats gently.

Reluctantly I comply.

Our guest, the eyes still dancing, offers no resistance as he is led into a private room. We are not permitted to follow as our presence might upset him, we are told. I look at my watch.

It is midnight. I am on my vacation time. The four of us settle into chairs and wait with mixed emotions for the sound of the doctor being throttled.

For two hours we sit. In my mind, I replay the moment when I lost my footing. It is like the nightmare of the fire all over. How many times in my sleep will I now bolt awake just before I fall?

Why am I not dead? I wonder.

Then, as I replay the moment on the bridge yet another time, the door opens abruptly. The doctor emerges.

We look up expectantly and in unison.

The doctor looks at the four of us disdainfully.

"Well . . . ?" Gary finally asks.

"There is nothing wrong with this man," the doctor says. "I'm discharging him."

One week after our chase across the Williamsburg Bridge I am lying in my camper in Ellenville. It is 7 A.M. on a beautiful morning in the mountains. I can hear birds and the joyful banter of my nieces and nephews outside. I can smell bacon and coffee being made.

I should get up. But I do not move.

I savor the gentle easing into wakefulness. A breeze ripples through my sleeping area. I puff up my pillow and steal a few more minutes of rest. I am still unwinding from the summer of eighty-one. When I return to work, I tell myself, it will be September. Things are usually calmer in September.

For the last few days, at odd moments such as this one, I have been thinking about life and death. I have been examining the strange circular pattern that events can take. In Vietnam a nameless soldier saved Sheppard's life. Sheppard saved Gary's. Gary saved mine. I'm old-fashioned. I believe such things happen for a reason. What is the reason that I remain alive? What is my purpose on this planet?

I think back to the circumstances that made a police officer out of me rather than a priest or a Franciscan brother. Someday I will no longer be a police officer, due to age or injury or who knows what.

Just before leaving for the Catskills I was with Tina, who pressed me on this very subject. I had to be honest.

"Suppose I got hurt badly," I said. "Suppose I couldn't be a cop anymore. You know I can't sit around. I'd have to be involved with people in some way."

"I understand that," she said.

"Well then, remember what I wanted to do with my life early on?" I asked. "Back when I was a teenager?"

She seemed stunned. "I thought you'd given that idea up. Entering the church."

"It's not the type of idea that just goes away," I answered.

"No," she said very slowly and thoughtfully. "I suppose it doesn't."

I do not like to dwell on my future. Instead, I like to find life's meaning as it is presented. But is there a man alive who does not at some moment reflect on his own mortality?

There is a saying we have in Emergency, one that may be incomprehensible to those whose jobs are more peaceful. *We can't get hurt,* we tell ourselves. *We are on a mission from God.* The truth is, no one on a life-and-death task wants to feel that he is alone.

I rise from bed. The youngsters greet me. Today Uncle Bill is going to take them on a hike through the far side of the mountain. They have not forgotten. Three boys from the Explorers' Post will come with us, as will my brother Jimmy.

MICHAEL

It is dark when Michael's flight arrives at Newark. He wanders the airport, not completely understanding that he is not in New York. Then a flight attendant directs him to the Path terminal at the airport. Michael has sixteen dollars in his pocket. He takes the PATH train to Manhattan.

Michael tries to talk to people on the street, but they keep walking. Back doors to restaurants, once the key to a dish-washing job, are locked. The traffic moves faster. The people are ruder and every door is bolted shut.

Even the police here seem less accessible. They walk in pairs or they ride in cars. And they eye him suspiciously.

Michael finds a meal on Houston Street in an all-night coffee shop full of cab drivers, winos, nodding youths in dark glasses, and loud young black women in short skirts. He wanders back toward Washington Square Park where he spends the night, fashioning a bed on a bench out of discarded newspapers.

The next day, there are no jobs. He can find no church group that will take him in. He wanders. He picks up a few dollars panhandling. But the following night is cooler. A park bench will not do. Rain is possible.

On East Broadway, near the Manhattan Bridge, Michael finds an abandoned car, the lock to its trunk torn off. He crawls into the trunk for the night, pulling it closed behind him for protection, then tying it in place from the inside. He leaves it open only enough for the passage of air.

That night it rains, but Michael remains dry. Still his rest is fitful. Always there are faceless voices, some of them angry, some of them crazy, wafting close to the car. At one point two men with a radio sit on the car's hood, drink beer, and

129

shout at each other in Spanish. New York was not like this in *King Kong*.

His third night in Manhattan, Michael discovers a better way to pass the hours of darkness. He rides the subways, nodding off a half hour here, forty minutes there, as the express trains thunder from one stop to the next. At many stations, the platforms are empty and warm. No one bothers him. A night's shelter courtesy of the New York Transit Authority costs only seventy-five cents or nothing at all if you jump the turnstile.

After a week, Michael finds work. He washes windows and dishes in the rear of a roach-infested luncheonette just off Mott Street in Chinatown. He receives a few dollars a day, plus meals.

Michael's co-worker is a stooped, bewhiskered black wino named Clarence. Clarence is in his early thirties and looks fifty-five. Clarence hit bottom early in life and knows his way around.

"The trouble is," Michael says to the whiskered tramp as they wash a pile of dishes in a steel sink filled with greasy lukewarm water, "I got a place to eat now. I got my three meals. But I don't have no place to stay."

"Gonna be early winter," says Clarence.

"Where can I stay cheap?" Michael asks more pointedly. "I been sleeping in the subways."

Clarence considers. "You got this hotel a few blocks from here," he says. "You can walk it in a few minutes. Costs three bucks and a quarter a night."

"What's it like?" Michael asks.

"It's a roof over your head. Who cares what else it's like?"

Clarence gives Michael the address. 101 Bowery. And the name of the recommended establishment is the Fulton Hotel.

Michael leaves work on a break later that same evening.

He goes to the address on the Bowery just below Houston Street. He sees the sign for the Fulton Hotel, an undistinguished six-story brick building but with people going and coming. When he enters, he is faced with a dirty stairway that smells of urine.

Though he hesitates, it is almost September now and Michael knows what anyone else who has ever drifted across America knows: September first is the date when the warm weather can turn against you.

Climbing the stairs, Michael encounters a pair of dozing men in a glass booth who manage the hotel. The room rates are posted behind them on a handlettered sign. There is a sitting area on the left, filled with broken, snoring men sprawled across battered, used chairs and sofas. Those men who are not sleeping either argue with each other, play cards, or stare forlornly out the Fulton's second-story window through a film of dirt.

"I want a room," Michael tells the men in the booth.

"You got money, son?"

"Yup." Michael shows him his wallet.

"You need a week's rent in advance."

Michael pays and is given a key to Room 312. He walks up and inspects a small five-by-twelve chamber equipped with a dented metal frame bed, an overhead light, a table, and a chair. He sees that the door will lock by key from the inside.

Then he tests the chair wedged under the doorknob where it will give him extra security at night. He is mildly satisfied. He has not had a secure night's sleep since leaving Cincinnati. The room is on the rear of the building. A cloudy window provides access to a rusting fire escape.

Michael goes back downstairs. He pauses at the glassed-in reception desk where the two men are now dozing again. He

131

then stares into the sitting area. Suddenly in one horrifying moment, Michael Buchanan's future and past intersect.

This is what he has come to. Skid Row. The Bowery. The Fulton is filled with forgotten men of all ages from all sections of the country. Their pasts are not unlike his own. True, they are older than Michael, but each shares with him the common afflictions of life on the road: no home, no family, no education, no money, no roots.

The sheer horror of it drops on the boy with a weight as heavy as the Fulton Hotel itself. A hopelessness engulfs him and he cries all night in his room. The next day he does not report to work but wanders the streets instead.

It is a sultry late afternoon on September first. Gary and I are at the Port Authority Bus Terminal scanning cubbyholes and peering under benches. We are looking for a bomb and we cannot find one. The dog handlers from the Bomb Squad are there and the dog has come up as empty as we have. We conclude that the threat, received by the Port Authority an hour ago, is unfounded. We leave hoping we haven't missed anything.

We are just getting back into our R.E.P. when we are called to an office building at Fifty-eighth and Madison on another bomb run and repeat the entire time-wasting, frustrating procedure once again.

"How was your vacation?" Gary asks me when we finish, not yet having had the opportunity to inquire.

"What vacation?" I ask.

Then we have an elevator extrication just around the corner on Fifty-seventh Street, eight flights above Dunhill Tailors. Six people are trapped, but the rescue is orderly. One woman is treated for mild hysteria. There are no injuries.

We drive downtown and have a quick sandwich at the Gray Table during what remains of our dinner hour. An Emergency man from the Bronx unit is amusing several of us with an account of how a former transit cop under F.B.I. surveillance went on a shooting spree at the precise moment that he was under surveillance.

"And what did the Feds do?" McCarthy asks.

"What do you think they did?" the Bronx E-man replies. "They turned tail and disappeared. Once the shooting started it wasn't their problem."

Everyone grins. Stories that embarrass other agencies are always popular at the Gray Table.

Captain Hanratty spots Gary and me as we are going back out.

"Hey," the captain says, "I got an important run for you two."

He motions to some papers and tucks them into a large envelope. "Can you get these over to Brooklyn?" he asks.

The papers are destined for Emergency Headquarters at Humbolt Street. They are the completed commendation forms for some character named Al Sheppard who will soon be adding to his lengthy collection of awards and citations.

"Let's toss them off the bridge as we drive to Brooklyn," I suggest to Gary, just loud enough for the ubiquitous Sheppard to hear.

We take the Williamsburg Bridge. As we drive, Gary and I both look up at the towers and suspension cables. Then, simultaneously, we catch each other and laugh.

"Nice night for a climb," I say to Gary, who is driving.

He shakes his head, as we glance up again. There isn't a man in our unit who doesn't scan towers and cables when he crosses a city bridge.

MICHAEL

Michael has now spent three nights in his room. Though he has cried a good deal, sobs are not strange to the Fulton, any more than screams or DT's.

Michael breaks the chain lock on the window and forces the old frame just enough so that he can crawl onto the fire escape where he begins to climb.

On the roof it is warm but there is a breeze. Standing on the tarpaper, Michael can see in all directions. He walks toward the front of the building, where he leans over a plaster and brick parapet and looks at the sidewalk.

He is crying now. Traffic passes slowly northward and southward on the Bowery. Down below, the pavement is cracked and uneven.

Summoning all his courage, Michael pulls himself up on the parapet. The bricks and masonry are a hundred years old. It quivers slightly. He swings one leg and tries to rally that final necessary effort.

Michael thinks of Texas and of Tennessee and of North Carolina. He thinks of his grandparents and of the pecan tree and of the dumplings on Sunday. He thinks of Memphis in May and of the mother he never knew and of his father.

His thoughts fix on his father. This is one way to defeat fate, he thinks. One plunge and it will all be over.

Gary and I are heading back toward Manhattan across the Brooklyn Bridge. It is 9:42 P.M. The city is a blaze of lights, the towers of the World Trade Center hulking skyward to our left and the constellations of midtown and of upper Manhattan on our right. Yet, magically, the heat of the day seems to have broken over the last few minutes. And the city is strangely quiet for a heartbeat or two.

Then our S.O.D. radio screeches to life. "ADAM ONE: CAN YOU GIVE US YOUR LOCATION?"

I grab the radiophone.

"Adam One to Central," I answer. "We're on the Brooklyn Bridge nearing Park Row. What have you got?"

"ADAM ONE: ANONYMOUS REPORT TO 911. REPORT OF A POSSIBLE JUMPER," Central tells us. "ONE-ZERO-ONE THE BOWERY. THE CROSS STREET IS HESTER."

Instinctively, Gary and I recall our last jumper. The whole episode with the madman on the Williamsburg Bridge flashes before us. Could this be our same crazed friend?

Twelve

G ARY puts his foot a little harder on the accelerator. We are coming off the bridge. The voice of the dispatcher crackles through the static.

"REPEAT, ADAM ONE: REPORT OF A POSSIBLE JUMPER AT ONE-ZERO-ONE THE BOWERY. CAN YOU TAKE IT?"

"This is Adam One, Central," I answer. "We can take it, but isn't Boy One closer?"

"Boy One is unaccounted for," answers the dispatcher. We have never met the voice on the other end of the radio. The dispatcher sits in an air-conditioned office at 101 Centre Street, handing out such fragments of information. There is now a pause of several seconds. Not a good sign.

"THAT'S A *CONFIRMED* JUMPER AT ONE-OH-ONE BOWERY, ADAM ONE. CAN YOU TAKE IT?"

"Ten four, Central," I answer. "Responding."

Gary hits the accelerator and the siren, and I hit the lights. We are on our way.

I know 101 Bowery, though I've never been inside the building. It's the Fulton Hotel, a high-class flop-house, a bit warmer, a bit safer, and maybe a shade cleaner than most of the fleabag places along the Bowery. The derelicts and hard-core losers who stay there are known to steal each other's clothes or maybe come out of the DT's swinging a broken bottle. Consequently, the residents sleep with their shoes under their pillow.

Gary and I cut our lights and siren as we arrive. A patrol car from the Fifth Precinct is already in front of the hotel. But the car is locked and no cops are in sight.

Already a crowd is forming.

Looking up, I see a thin, dark-haired boy sitting on the brick parapet that projects slightly over the facade of the building. One of his legs is hanging over the side. I count the windows going up. There are six. Six flights to climb; I hope I'll get there before the boy jumps.

Reaching back into the van, I pick up the radio again and call central.

"Adam One confirming potential suicide at One-Oh-One Bowery. The individual is a white teenage male on the rooftop. Roll the big truck and get a supervisor. Request an airbag and a back-up."

"TEN FOUR," Central replies. "NOTIFYING."

Gary is moving toward the rear door of our van while I lock the cab. On the roof, the boy has not moved.

We are buckling our Morrissey belts—which have steel loops to be joined with a lifeline—as we run into the building. The odor of the hallway, with its litter of food wrappers, bottles, and beer cans, is overpowering. We step around the trash, Gary half a step behind me with the lifeline—100 feet of heavy rope that can be so important in any operation such as this. We pace ourselves as we climb the stairs; no use arriving out of breath. Even so, my heart has started to pound as we come to the top floor. Another dingy flight to the roof.

"Easy, Billy, easy," Gary says.

The battered old door swings open onto a tarpaper roof.

It is 9:53. We have made it in just eleven minutes.

The first thing we see are two uniformed cops—rookies from the Fifth Precinct. Fresh faces. New uniforms. One of them nods toward the boy on the ledge. There is also a uniformed detective specialist, Jack Brady. He and the two rookies had been on a training patrol when the anonymous call came into 911.

"Okay. What's going on?" I ask.

"I can't get much out of him," Brady answers softly, giving half a glance toward the boy. "I think his name is Michael Thompson; he says he's from New Jersey."

I hear sirens and can see reflections of flashing lights. That means our back-up team from Emergency Service is arriving.

Brady retreats a few steps. The job is now ours.

The boy is nervously watching us from about fifty feet away. He is thin and his dark hair is a mess. He wears a blue T-shirt that, ironically, appears to say FIGHT ME. He is crying. I guess that he might be fifteen years old.

The boy is alert to my every move, yet my only fear is for him.

I feel the sweat gathering under my shirt. The ledge where the boy sits is elevated about three feet from the roof and, to make things difficult, the parapet leans slightly outward.

I draw a breath while Gary looks for something solid to lash the lifeline to, something that won't give an inch even if all three of us go over the side. He tests a brick chimney. It's solid. He loops the lifeline around the chimney and ties the line securely. The boy watches apprehensively.

138

"How you doing?" I say to the kid. He continues to cry and doesn't answer. His attention is on Gary, who will have to try him first.

"Hey, look, it can't be all that bad," Gary says. I stand behind him and take a loose grip on the lifeline attached to his Morrissey belt.

The boy looks away, distracted for a moment by whatever is going on in the street below. Undoubtedly the crowd is growing. I can hear a commotion down there even though I can't see anything.

Gary and I steal a few feet forward. The boy looks back suddenly and we freeze. "Hey, I know you're upset," Gary says. "Take it easy. We're here to help you." The boy watches Gary but doesn't answer. He looks like a decent kid but he won't speak. Not a good sign.

The boy shifts his weight, and for a splint second I think he's going. I exhale a long breath when I realize he's still there.

Something happens below, the boy glances down again, and we pick up another few feet. He looks back quickly, as though he'd been testing us. The closer we get, the more terrified and distraught he seems.

"Take it easy," Gary says again. "How are you doing?"

The boy glances at Gary. Still no answer.

"Can we get you anything?" Gary asks. "A cigarette? Coffee? A beer?"

Any offer that is accepted will establish a tiny rapport, and will also buy us some time.

"I don't want anything," the boy says, shaking his head. Now that he's talking to us I am surprised to pick up a Southern accent. We creep a few inches forward, and Gary asks, "What's wrong? Who's hassling you?"

The boy turns on us. "Leave me alone, will ya!" he cries out.

"Okay, okay!" Gary says, raising his hands to placate the boy. We make the motion of retreating but actually move back very little. "I'm going to stay over here," Gary promises him, designating an imaginary line at his feet. "I'm not moving."

Gary has taken his shot, and the chemistry isn't there. I draw a breath. It's my turn now.

"Michael?" I begin by trying the name that Brady gave me. "My name is Bill and my partner's name is Gary. Please, I want you to listen to me."

The crying hasn't stopped. But he looks over.

"Mike?" I ask, "that's your name, isn't it? Mike?"

"Yeah, that's my name."

"How old are you, Mike?" I ask.

"Seventeen."

I take him at his word, though he looks younger. He starts crying harder.

"Hey, Mike, take it easy," I say. "Let's talk for a while."

He doesn't say no.

"How long have you been in New York?"

He doesn't answer.

"Where you been living?"

"Around," he says.

"Just around? Around where?"

He shrugs.

"You been living on the streets?" I ask.

He nods very slightly. He is looking down toward the airbag that is now being set up. Gary and I creep forward.

"Where were you living before that?"

"New Jersey," he answers.

I know from his accent that he is not from there originally.

"What about your parents?" I ask. "Where are they?"

He shrugs.

"Is your father home?"

"My father was an alcoholic," Mike says. "He beat me. He never cared about me."

I've dealt with kids enough to smell when they are lying. And I don't smell it here.

"Where's your father now?" I ask carefully.

"I don't know where he is and I don't care! He doesn't care. Nobody cares."

He is sobbing so hard now that I can barely distinguish what he is saying. Something about wanting to get a decent job and an education. I pick up on that. "Did you finish high school, Mike?"

"No."

"What school did you go to?"

The words come more easily.

"I went to Freedom High School."

"Where's that, Mike?"

"North Carolina."

"But didn't you say you were from New Jersey," I gently remind him.

"I was living there for a while," he replies.

"Oh? Who were you living with?"

"Friends."

I wait, knowing there is more to come.

"One of my friends, he died. That's where I got this shirt. That's why I'm wearing this shirt."

Because he's sitting at an angle, I can't see what it says.

"Show me," I say. "Let me see."

He holds his chest toward me. It does not say FIGHT ME, as I'd earlier thought, but FIGHT MD.

I ask him what the letters mean.

"Fight Muscular Dystrophy," he says. "A friend of mine. His name was Andy. He was twelve years old, and this summer he died of muscular dystrophy. He was an altar boy. He died and I went to the funeral."

"I'm sorry, Mike. It's tough to lose a friend. I've lost plenty of friends. But still you've got to go on, you know."

"No," he says. "I don't have to. Because nobody cares."

"I care, Mike."

Pressing him to continue, all I get at times is more sobs. While I work at keeping up a conversation, Gary again offers to get him a sandwich or a beer. Mike refuses, but he doesn't quit talking.

He keeps telling me that he doesn't want to turn out like his father, that he wants to finish high school—at a real high school, not at some night school.

I find myself responding to all this. After my own father died prematurely in 1964, I tell him, I'd quit school and wound up working as an electrician's apprentice. But I'd wanted a high school diploma and so I went back and got mine at night. And I do understand what Michael means about not wanting to do that.

I get him to talk about school. I learn he's weak in math— just as I was—and that he likes English. When I confess to him that I was very bad at spelling, he looks at me hard for a second. When pressed, he admits that he likes to write some- times. I assure him that he is probably better at it than I'll ever be, and he gives me a half shrug. Do I see the vaguest trace of a smile? Or is it wishful thinking?

Finally I ask him to tell me about the people he's been living with.

Fragments of his history come tumbling out as if they have

been exploding inside him. He hasn't seen his mother since he was two, and doesn't remember her. He says he was taken away from his father by a Tennessee family court in 1972. After that he says, it was one foster home to another—most of them bad. He tells how he ran away, drifting north until he landed here. I never take my eyes off him. Time is passing very quickly now.

Two back-up officers from Manhattan Emergency Services have arrived, and taken positions about ten feet behind Gary and me. From a different location, Frank Heller, who will be in charge of coordinating our moves with the moves of the officers on the street, has also arrived.

Mike is looking down toward the street and crying loudly.

"I don't want to turn out to be an uneducated bum," he says, a theme he keeps coming back to. "But nobody cares."

I grope for a subject as Gary and I move a little closer. I ask him if he likes music. At first he doesn't answer. Bad sign again. Then, with more prodding, he mentions the Bee Gees.

We discuss the Bee Gees and other pop groups for several minutes. Then down goes his head. I seem to be running out of words. Gary and I are still much too far away to try for a grab. Michael makes no move, but the way he is sitting, with one leg on each side of the parapet, I know he doesn't have forever.

I glance at my watch. It is 10:37. We have been inching forward for three-quarters of an hour.

I go back to what seems to be his greatest concern—getting an education.

"Mike, look," I begin. "I can get you into a high school. If that's what you want, I can get you in."

"No, you won't," he sobs. "That's just cop talk! You're just feeding me a line!"

I steal a few inches closer as he wipes his eyes, but verbally I've gotten nowhere. I change the subject. "You like to hunt or fish?" I ask.

"Yeah. Sometimes."

So I tell him bout the cabin I have in the Catskill Mountains, near Ellenville. He seems to be listening and I go on talking for several minutes about the place—the wild game up there and the camping grounds. But now I've lost his attention. A bright light is shining from the street.

"What the hell is going on down there?" I mutter to Gary.

Gary mumbles something into the walkie-talkie and tells me, "They've got a crowd of about 150 people," he says. "Plus television." Well, hot dog, we're making the news. It crosses my mind that the footage they really want is not a rescue but a suicide. Better ratings. Then I dismiss the idea. Anyhow, it's not my concern. My job is to get close enough for the grab. Nothing else.

Michael is still crying. He is positioned in such a way that it is impossible to sneak anyone in behind him.

Suddenly, from down below, there is a wave of intensely bright light sweeping up. It is the television crew doing their job, but it threatens to sabotage our entire operation. Michael is blinded by it. Moving his arms to cover his eyes, he nearly loses his balance. I use the instant to advance slightly, yet my heart nearly stops as I see Michael shifting his weight.

A voice near me yells, "Turn it off! Turn that goddamn thing off!" It is Gary. I almost laugh. Does he think they can hear him on the street? Now he grabs his walkie-talkie. "Shut off the bastard with that light!" he barks. Seconds later the light is off. Michael is staring down. Almost two hundred people are staring back up. Traffic is stopped in both directions. There are more than twenty cops in uniform, an airbag, two police trucks, and four cars below; and on the roof Michael is cornered by seven of us inching closer to him. Who wouldn't be terrified? Why should he trust me or anyone else? I feel for the kid.

"Mike," I say, "look at me." I have now edged to within eight feet of the parapet. He looks at me. But now an isolated voice from the crowd across the street calls out. "Jump!" There is a smattering of approval from the rest of the crowd. Some other dumb bastard joins in: "Jump!" Isolated at first, the voices become a refrain.

"Jump! Jump!"

Mike stares down at the street. We have been on the roof an hour and twenty minutes, Gary and I, building his trust. And this profane mob is about to steal him from us.

"Jesus Christ!" I mutter. "Can't somebody shut them up?" Gary is already on the radio. "We're going to lose him if we can't shut the crowd up!"

We manage to move another half step closer. I implore Mike to talk to me.

He does, but I don't like what I hear.

"You see? They don't care. Nobody cares. I'm nothing but a statistic."

"Don't listen to them, Mike," I beg him. "Listen to me. I'm the one who's been up here talking to you. You're not talking to them, it's me you're talking to."

"Oh, it's just cop talk."

"No, Mike, it's not. Believe me. You've only just gotten here. Things can really be different."

"Once I jump and hit that sidewalk, it's all over," he tells me. "I got no more problems."

He watches me intently. He must know his bluff is being called.

145

With a quick movement his other foot is over the ledge.

"Jump! Jump!" the crowd is chanting again. It's as if, for the first time in his life, he can please a lot of people at once.

When I try to move forward, he shouts, "Don't come near me!"

The palms of my hands are soaking wet. "Mike, I can't see you wasting your life," I tell him. "I know you want a high school diploma. I'll see that you get one."

"How are you going to get me one?" He is crying again.

"I can get you into a school, believe me, I know I can do it."

"I don't want any equivalency diploma," he sobs. "I want a real diploma, from a decent school."

The crowd down below is quieter now.

"Mike, I can get you into Curtis High School in Staten Island," I promise him. "It's a good school. I went there myself and I know they'll take you." His expression worries me but I am still seven feet away so I keep talking.

"As far as a room is concerned, Mike, I got a six-room house. I got a spare room in my own house and it's gathering dust. I'll give you that room. It's yours to stay in. I can't see you wasting your life, Mike. Not over things that are so small. Things you can have."

"It's just cop talk," he repeats. "You're just saying that. You don't care. Nobody cares."

"Michael, you're wrong," I say again. "I care. I mean everything I'm telling you. I'd be proud to have a boy like you as my son. I don't want to see you waste your life."

He seems to be slightly calmer, but is breathing hard. And I am close enough to see the terror and confusion, the fear and the friendlessness in his eyes.

Gary and I gain half a step as he wipes a hand across his face.

146

Gary speaks now, in a measured voice so the cops behind us can hear.

"Billy, you know that job we were going to do yesterday? I think we should go do it *now*." On the word "now" the two of us bolt forward. I lunge for the boy's waist, and Gary grabs him by the shoulders.

The parapet quivers at the impact, as the boy fights back out of some instinct triggered by fear and surprise. Our back-ups are on us like a couple of bears and grab the three of us, pulling us back onto the roof.

We have him pinned, his arms secured. We have him.

Now, still crying, he shrieks at me. "Well, what about it? Did you mean what you said?"

"I meant what I said, Mike."

"You're going to keep your promises?"

"I keep my promises, Mike."

He says little as Gary and I take him down the six flights and bring him out into the glare of the television lights. The same people who were chanting *Jump! Jump!* now give us an ovation. Near the door to the Fulton is the ambulance that will take Michael to Bellevue Hospital. Gary and I ease him into the back of it and I say to him, "Hang on, Mike. It's going to be all right for you."

"Sure," he sobs. He is looking at me as he sits beside the attendant in the rear of the ambulance. I hold the door open a moment longer. Our eyes meet, and I close the door. As I watch the vehicle pull away, Gary pats me on the shoulder. "Good job, Chief," he says, beginning to unhook his Morrissey belt. "Come on, time to pick up." He exhales a long, tired breath.

"You know," I say, "there's something we got to do."

"What?"

"You heard what I said up on the roof."

Gary looks at me sympathetically. "Hey, Billy...? How long you been on this job? What's on the roof is finished. It's out of our hands now." The ambulance has just turned the corner onto Houston Street. I look after it and then back at Gary.

"This one's different," I tell him. "We got to go to Bellevue. I want to check out the kid's story and see how he's doing."

Gary rolls his eyes and begins putting our equipment back into the van. There is no further discussion. I know that when our shift is over an hour from now he will go with me uptown to Bellevue.

Thirteen

SEPTEMBER first has just become September second. Gary and I are off duty. We are bound once again for Bellevue Psychiatric, this time to look for Michael.

I ponder the possible irony of having to deal with the same psychiatrist as we did after the Williamsburg Bridge incident. "There's nothing wrong with this boy," I imagine the same doctor saying. Then where does he go? Back to another roof?

We see a familiar face, Officer Frank Rivera, who filled in the AIDED card for Michael at Bellevue. Frank sends us down a corridor to a waiting room. There we find Michael. He is sitting in a wheelchair. He wears a hospital gown. His face looks even more drawn, thin, and frightened than I remember.

He looks up and at first we are just two guys in uniform. Then a look of surprise crosses his face as he recognizes us.

"Mike," I say to him as I walk over. "How you doing?"

"Okay, I guess."

"How they treating you?"

"They want to ask me a whole bunch of questions." Michael drawls with his Southern inflection. "Psychiatrists," he shrugs, "Crazier than their patients." He draws a long breath. "They gave me a meal here at least. I guess the place is good for something."

"I didn't hurt you up there, did I?" I ask. "I know we grabbed you pretty hard."

"No. I'm okay." He looks at us conspiratorially. "Can I ask you guys for something?"

"Shoot."

"Either of you got a cigarette?"

Neither Gary nor I smoke. So we bum a smoke from another cop and pass it on to Michael. "They won't give me cigarettes here," Michael says.

"It's a hospital, after all," Gary reminds him.

"Yeah. Sure thing," Michael says, looking at us with suspicion. "The doctors smoke, too, you know. Specially the shrinks."

"They're your lungs," I tell him.

He takes the cigarette and sticks it in his mouth. A nurse provides a match. Michael inhales deeply and blows out a long stream of smoke. "Why are you guys here?" he asks. "You got to fill out some reports?"

"All that stuff you told me on the roof," I say, "about your family, those foster homes, those institutions. I want to know how much was bull."

"Does it matter?" he asks.

"Yes."

He thinks. "Maybe one percent," he gives me a sly smile. "I tell tales sometimes, and sometimes I forget details. But I was telling you pretty much the gospel tonight," he adds. "What about you?"

"I was telling you the truth," I tell him. "I'll get you into a school. And if you need a home, or a good place to stay, I can find you one."

He looks at me and I see both the hope and the skepticism within his eyes. He wants to believe me, but he doesn't dare.

Then he looks at his feet. He glances back up and studies our uniforms. "In the past cops have never done anything but lock me up, take me to reform schools, sit me down in court, and put me in foster homes," he says slowly. "Why should things be any different here?"

I look him straight in the eye. "For one very simple reason, Mike," I say. "Gary and I have finished our shift for the night. We should be on our way home to get some sleep. But we're not. We're here."

"Sure, you're here," he says. "But I know how the system works for people like me. There's nothing you can do about it. You'll see."

An orderly appears and moves slowly to the rear of Michael's chair. "I have to take this patient in now," he says.

Michael snuffs out the end of his cigarette, saving the rest for later. He puts it in the pocket of his gown.

"See you sometime," he says.

I put my hand on the orderly's to halt the chair. "I'm going to check your story, Mike," I tell the boy. "I want to see what I can do for you."

He says nothing.

"Who should I talk to? Where should I call?"

I take out my notebook and write down some of the names, places, and institutions that Mike first mentioned on the roof. I fill an entire page. Then he admits that his real name is Buchanan.

He looks curiously at my hands as I write. Then I close the book.

"I'll be in touch," I tell him.

I offer my hand. There's a moment's hesitation, he takes it. We shake. "See you," he says.

Gary shakes hands with him, too. The orderly wheels him toward the examination room. We watch. Then Michael turns quickly in the chair and looks at us, almost as if to see if we are still there. We are. "Hey, Bill?" he says. The orderly stops the chair.

"Yeah?"

He gives us a big grin. "Thanks."

I am at the Gray Table the next afternoon, waiting for my shift to start. I have little to say. I am thinking about Michael and the system that apparently failed him so badly. I'm sure that Michael is a decent kid. Cops develop a certain sense about children. You can tell a troubled good kid from a punk just by looking.

Tommy McCarthy walks by. "You're gonna make this whole squad famous, Fox," he says. "Who the hell do you think you are? You just came into Emergency. It's the older guys who should be making us famous, don't you think?"

"Whatever you say, Tommy," I answer.

McCarthy's hard-edged humor is not completely in jest. He drops a copy of the New York *Post* on the table in front of me. The *Post* seems to be required afternoon reading in our precinct these days.

The headline screams, JUMP! JUMP! I glance at the story inside and marvel at how simple it all seems afterward. A couple of cops spent a few hours on a flophouse roof, talking a scared kid out of taking his life, appealing to him to listen to them and not to the irresponsible mob below.

The pictures include several of me and Gary carrying Michael out. I read further. The publicity is fine for the squad. I am bothered only that the news media missed part of the point. It wasn't just Gary and me on the roof doing some quick talking. The whole rescue—like any rescue—was a team effort. Every cop there, including the precinct guys in crowd control, deserved part of the credit.

"You're not going to believe this," Gary says as he pulls up to the table, sliding into a chair beside me. "Remember last night when the crowd started chanting? Remember when we radioed down to try to get them to shut up?"

I nod.

"Well, one of our men turned to a couple of guys chanting the loudest, those two big fat guys with suits and ties who got out of a car from New Jersey."

"Yeah?" I ask expectantly.

"This cop from the Five Precinct says to them in particular, 'The next guy who shouts something, I'm going to knock his teeth out.'"

"Good for him," I say. "Something shut up those irresponsible loudmouths. So it worked."

"Yeah," Gary says, "it worked. But this morning the same two loudmouths walked into the Fifth Precinct and wanted to file a complaint against the cop for being rude to them. Can you believe it?"

For my entire shift this day I fight a rear guard battle with my common sense. Every cop in the city knows better than to get personally involved in cases. I even know better myself.

Once a few years ago I was trying to help a Staten Island kid who'd been in and out of trouble with the police. I helped keep him in school. I helped find him a job. I tried to be available when he needed someone to talk to. I did well with him for a few weeks. Then one day he came to my place to thank me.

We had a nice chat. He said he was thirsty so I sent him to the refrigerator for some beer. He came back with a couple of cans and we talked some more. Then he thanked me again and left.

I felt pretty good about it until I discovered that a hundred dollars was missing from an envelope my mother kept in the kitchen.

Call me naive or a fool, but then explain to me what good it is to carry a badge and represent the public order if you aren't willing to step into a critical situation and try to help.

So much for the battle with my common sense. I complete an uneventful four-to-twelve shift with Gary during which I am uncharacteristically quiet. I think back on everything I ever learned in my religious instruction and everything I've learned as a cop. Life is rarely a series of easy decisions. But I already know what I must do.

Fourteen

I am sitting in an office in Bellevue that belongs to an attractive woman in her mid-thirties. She is the social worker initially assigned to Michael's case. "I wish I could be more optimistic," Helen Mayron says to me. "But I know too well how this system works. I know what you're going to be up against."

She is leafing through a preliminary report on Michael made at the hospital. She also has some sealed reports from the various child welfare agencies in Tennessee.

"I promised Michael," I say to her, "that if all else fails he can come to my house. I want to know how I can keep that promise."

She arches her eyebrows. "Are you certain it's a promise you should have made?" she asks.

"Yes."

Helen Mayron is doing her job.

155

She cannot be certain of my intentions. She asks sound questions. Do I make enough money to support a foster son? How will my mother, a woman in her late sixties, be able to cope with the arrival of a troubled teenager? How can I provide a parental figure if I'm away at work so much of each day?

"Most fathers work, don't they?" I ask.

"Yes," she answers. "But you're single. The adoption or foster care agencies want to see a family unit of some sort. Please understand, Mr. Fox. I want to help Michael, also. But I know what's going to happen. These agencies are not going to be gentle with you."

I smile. "If it's necessary to help Michael," I tell her, "I won't be gentle with them, either."

She smiles too and I feel that she is an ally, even though she does not have the authority to place a child in a foster home. The New York State Child Placement Service does that.

"So what's going to happen to Michael?" I ask. "They've got him under observation for two weeks. Nobody can see him except other doctors."

She closes the files. "Michael is seventeen with a history of petty crime and psychological problems. He's an abused child and yet he's almost a young man. Let's just say it would be unusual if any family opened up to him."

"So then he becomes a ward of the state, right?" She nods. "But which state?"

"Technically," she says, "Tennessee should take him back. But I spoke to the Tennessee agency this morning. They claim he's North Carolina's problem. So I called North Carolina."

"And they said he's Tennessee's problem," I surmised.

"Almost. North Carolina said he's our problem. New York. *We* have him, so he's *our* problem."

I start to feel myself burn. How many times have I seen

156

serious crimes committed by kids whose names were shuffled around on lists? Too many.

"So let me get this straight," I say. "Tennessee and North Carolina won't take him back. Bellevue's not prepared to keep him for more than two weeks and child welfare in New York 'probably' won't let me file for adoption."

She nods. "And even if they let you file, even if you fight with them tooth and nail, it will take months. You know how it is. Psychological tests. Character studies. Endless interviews." She shrugs the shrug of a woman who knows the system too well to have any respect for it. "Meanwhile, Michael has to be somewhere. So you and I both know what that means."

"Spofford?" I ask.

She nods and I wince at the thought. Spofford Youth Center is the end of the line for juvenile offenders in New York City. It is populated by fifteen-year-old career criminals ranging from car thieves to killers. It is a hell hole and everyone knows it. Yet it is now the only institution to which Michael can be sent. I would sooner see him back on the streets.

"They'd hold him in Spofford until his eighteenth birthday next March. Then, if he hasn't run away yet, they'll simply release him," she says.

I glance at my watch. It is 3 P.M. and I must be getting to my job.

"Doesn't it make more sense," I ask, "to let him stay in my home? Even if it's on a temporary basis until something better opens for him? At least he can go to school like any other kid."

"Of course it makes more sense, Mr. Fox," she tells me. "But the system doesn't respond to sense. It responds to its own rules." She picks up a pencil and opens the file again.

157

"I'll put down that there's the possibility of a home with you if nothing else can be found. That might help. But don't get your hopes up. I shouldn't get Michael's hopes up, either."

"I understand."

"If I were you," she concludes, "I'd be persistent, play by the rules, and keep your eyes open for some little quirk in the system. That's really the best you can hope for."

I nod and she sets down the pencil.

"If you wish to pursue this," she says, "you'll have to go to Child Placement next. Good luck."

I hit some traffic on Twenty-fourth Street and my usual parking lot is full. I circle the block and finally park near the East Side Drive and half-run, half-jog to the precinct.

I race up the steps to the locker room, past the plaque in memory of Patrick O'Connor and past Paulie Redecha, the jolly blue giant in full uniform, who stands by the captain's room reading a psychology textbook. Paulie is studying for a Bachelor's degree from New York Tech. How he finds time, I'll never know.

Paulie glances at his watch as I race by, three minutes on the safe side of being late. He says nothing, just looks at me and his watch. Some psychologist.

I stand near my locker, tearing off my clothes and climbing into the uniform. Gary, already dressed, comes by. "Where you been?" he asks.

"I had some things to do."

He notes the vagueness of my answer. "Oh. Some 'things.' More important than coming to work, huh?" Gary is reproachful. Our job calls for concentration and attention. We should not be racing in the door three minutes before roll call. I am yanking on my shirt and clipping on my tie.

"Hey?" Gary asks again. "What's the matter with you? You got problems today? Some sort of trouble?" There is a friendly concern in his voice.

"I'm okay. Gare. No problem."

"You're in here but your head isn't." He motions to my locker. "You forgot your vest."

I see it hanging there. The guys laugh as I remove shirt and tie and hastily put on my bullet-proof vest. The sergeant who should be calling roll walks by to see what the commotion is about, and then takes a long, long drink of water from the cooler, affording me just enough time to beat him back to the squad room for roll.

We take an easy shift. No heavy jobs. Gary asks me if I've talked to Michael and I tell him that Michael is being held without outside contact for two weeks. But I do not mention Helen Mayron or the conversation we have just had at Bellevue. I wonder if my partner has any suspicions of what is running through my head.

It is midnight when we return to the precinct. I am tired. Captain Hanratty has a present for me on his desk. "What the hell's this?" I ask when Sgt. Lewis hands it to me.

"Fan mail," he said. There are about a dozen envelopes held together by a rubber band. Some of the letters carry my full name, others just say, OFFICER FOX, NEW YORK CITY POLICE. I begin to open them as Gary looks over my shoulder.

Something gets tight inside my chest. These are letters from average people—people like myself—who were moved by the squad's rescue of Michael and by Michael's plight. They congratulate Gary and me on our work. And, surprisingly, several enclose cash and checks. A Pennsylvania woman writes, "God bless you, Mr. Fox. Please accept this $8 check to help Michael in some way."

We have received a total of ninety-six dollars for this boy we barely know.

"We can't accept money," Gary reminds me. "We put any of that stuff into our lockers and we can be busted from the force."

"But it's not for us. It's for Michael."

We find our solution the next morning. Gary and I go to a P.B.A. attorney and tell him what is happening. With his assistance, we open a trust account for Michael Buchanan's welfare and education. Gary and I chip in ten dollars to open the account, and two days later we start depositing the checks. A few more letters arrive each day. Apparently that JUMP! JUMP! appeared in several newspapers. The generosity of some people overwhelms me. And the money, while certainly not a fortune, starts to add up.

"Well," I say to my mother and sister over lunch the next day, "at least Mike's not broke anymore. Even if he doesn't know it."

"Just tell me this, Billy," my mother says, "when are you bringing him home?"

I look up and see Eileen suppressing a laugh.

"Bringing who home?" I protest. "I didn't say anything about bringing Mike to the house."

"Don't be silly," she says with the intuition gained from having raised three sons who became police officers. "Mike's welcome here. And shame on you. After all these years, don't you realize that I always know what you're thinking?"

By telephone, I finally reach a Mr. Lerrick at City Placement who does everything he can to discourage me from getting involved. He suggests that I should be disqualified from getting Michael by virtue of being single and assures me that any procedure to gain custody of Michael will take weeks, maybe

160

months. He also warns me that if I do manage to circumvent the system and somehow gain custody of Michael, I will have disqualified myself from receiving any state money for foster care.

"I'm not in this for the money," I tell him.

"Actually, that's my next question, Mr. Fox," he says. "What *is* in this for you?"

"I'm trying to help a kid no one else wants to help," I snap back.

"But why this kid? There's ten thousand kids in the street who need help. You know that."

"I made promises to Michael," I tell him.

"Well," he continues helpfully, "you probably shouldn't have. Look, you're a cop. You should know better than to get personally involved in a case like this."

I do not like Mr. Lerrick. I do not want to hear why things cannot be done. I want to know how this *can* be accomplished.

"I want the name of your superior," I say to him, "and I want the name of the psychiatrist handling Michael's case at Bellevue."

"That's not going to help you."

"You can give them to me over the phone or I can come over and get them from you. Take your pick."

He gives me the names.

I now call Lerrick's superior and hear more of the same. I hang up angrily after speaking to the man, wondering if his agency ever helps anyone. Helen Mayron's words echo in my ears: Look for a quirk in the system. I am looking, I am looking.

By the time I reach Dr. Eugene Farber at Bellevue Psychiatric his is the tenth voice-on-the-phone that morning. He is also the doctor assigned to Michael's case.

I identify myself.

161

"Oh, yes, of course. Officer Fox. I read about you in the papers."

"Yeah, we got pretty good coverage," I laugh. So does he. Dr. Farber sounds like a decent man. I cross my fingers.

"That was quite a rescue," he says.

"The press made a big thing of it because there was a crowd there," I say. "Stuff like that goes on all the time."

Then I realize: He is sounding me out with small talk. He is letting me do the talking. So I move to the point. "How's Michael?" I ask.

There is a silence on the line, a pause that I don't like. "He's having his problems," Dr. Farber tells me. "But considering what he's been through, it's not entirely unexpected."

"What type of problems?"

"I'm not permitted to tell you."

"Is he still in the same ward?"

"No."

"You moved him?"

"The patient was moved, yes."

"Is he still at Bellevue?" I press, growing increasingly alarmed.

"He's still at Bellevue," Dr. Farber says. "And he's in a ward where we can keep a closer eye on him."

"Hey, doc, look," I tell him, my Irish starting to flare up again. "I been in those wards of yours and I know that no one gets moved without a reason. I'm not going to interfere with whatever you're doing, but I've got a vested interest in Michael. No one else is calling you from the outside about him, so come on. Level with me."

"I'm sorry, but—"

"Don't you understand. I'm just trying to stay in a position to help the kid."

162

I hear him exude a long breath, not so much in annoyance as from fatigue.

"Come on, doc," I ask. "Please. We're both trying to give the kid a break."

It works. "There are two developments in Michael's case," he says. "One is favorable and one is not so good."

"Yeah?"

"We may have an eventual home for him. A couple from Westchester county read about Michael in the papers. They're filing for adoption. They've always wanted a son and they're willing to take in a teenager."

I am stunned—at once overjoyed at Michael's prospects and disappointed for my own. Dr. Farber describes the couple as being from a prosperous suburb. The potential foster father is in his late fifties and his wife is about forty. They have money, the right credentials, and a good home. This sounds promising.

"So what's the unfavorable development?" I ask.

"Michael is in isolation in a special twenty-four-hour intensive observation ward," the doctor tells me. "Michael's still a very disturbed boy. He tried to commit suicide again. He slashed his wrists."

Later that same week, I meet Dr. Farber for the first time. My intuitions are correct. He is a good man doing a good job. He is doing his work by the book and is protecting and caring for his patient. What worries me is not Dr. Farber but the system.

"Michael comes out of isolation in six more days," Dr. Farber tells me, "and then I don't know what we can do. The state will want to move him."

"Spofford?"

"Let's worry about that when the time comes," he says.

Dr. Farber introduces me to George and Ruth Blaylock who live in Westchester. They have been following Michael's case since they first read about it in the newspapers. This morning they have filed a preliminary application with Child Placement. Not only do they wish to adopt Michael, but they are exactly what Child Placement claims to be looking for. George Blaylock speaks enthusiastically about meeting Michael and bringing home a son. Mrs. Blaylock sits quietly in Dr. Farber's office, listening to her husband. I wish the Blaylocks luck. I know they will be awarded Michael before I will.

Gary is out with the flu. I am working with Joe Bregman, Tommy McCarthy's usual partner. It is night in lower Manhattan and a crowd is already gathering around the body in the street. The reflection of the flashing red light from our truck leaps from the bakery window behind the stricken man.

"He's dead," says a nearby newsstand owner. "Just get him out of here."

But the man is moaning. I feel the pulse at his throat and I loosen the filthy shirt and tattered jacket. The heartbeat is very faint and his face is ashen. I take a good look at his unfocused eyes. Bregman just stands and stares.

"We're gonna have to do C.P.R. on him," I tell my partner.

"Are you kidding? It's a fucking wino."

My head snaps up. I have no patience for him or his old-school street-cop attitudes. "No, I ain't kidding!" I explode. "He's alive."

"I'll call the ambulance."

"I can't do the whole C.P.R. by myself, Bregman!" I call to him. "Come on! Give me a fucking hand!"

"I'll give you a hand but I'm not puffing any air into no wino."

164

I do not have time to think, only to react, as the man's heartbeat is almost gone. I spread a plastic liner across the man's face and I press my mouth toward the liner. I exhale. I try to blow hard into the man's lungs, to keep his body working.

In the back of my mind I wonder if I should blame Joe Bregman. The wino reeks of urine, sweat, and whiskey. Yet he is human. I am not trying to be a hero. I am only trying to do what I'm paid for.

Bregman keeps the crowd back. I am aware of their taunts and their smart-ass remarks. I would like to ask them if mouth-to-mouth would seem as funny if they were lying on the sidewalk, their lives slipping away.

I can hear the ambulance approaching. I am growing dizzy from the incessant, hard puffing and blowing into the dying man's mouth. The attendants jump out of their vehicle. They have a stretcher and they press oxygen to the man's face as I move my own head away and gasp for air.

I am dizzy and sweating like a pig. I feel the flood of perspiration running down my back under the bullet-proof vest.

"He's in bad shape," I gasp to the attendants. But they have two eyes. They can see that, too. I look at Bregman, standing near the R.E.P. I would like to punch him, but I do not.

"The heart's gone," one of the meds says. "Get the defibrillators."

We press the electric panels to the man's chest and his whole body jumps as the initial voltage shoots into him. We try again. We pound on the chest. Bregman is jumping in to help us now. Some Fifth Precinct men set the perimeter. We have done everything we could, but the man is dead.

As I get to my feet I have a strange sensation about this place. I look to my left and I see the Fulton Hotel. 101 Bowery. I look up toward the parapets. Nobody up there tonight.

165

"That man was dead as a mackeral when we arrived," Bregman continues to argue as we return to the precinct an hour later. "I'm not giving C.P.R. to no dead wino."

"Who are you giving C.P.R. to?" I demand, following him up the steps to the locker room. Our dispute is so intense by now that everyone is stopping to watch. "What are you going to do? Take your pick? A guy looks clean, you give it to him? A girl looks nice, you give it to her? But no old people, maybe? How about Italians or blacks or Jews or Hispanics? Where do you draw your goddamned line?"

"Dry up, will you Fox," he says. "You want to be the big hero by puffing up bums, that's fine! But I been on this job thirteen years and I'm looking for another seven. I'm not busting my chops over some dead bum."

"It's not just a dead bum, Bregman. It's your whole frigging attitude toward the job! You either do the whole job or you don't do the job at all. You don't pick and choose."

"Fox, you and Gary can do the job any way you see fit. Tommy and I will do ours the way we've always done it. We don't need you to tell us."

There are no other voices in the squad room other than Johnny Carson's coming across the television. Men leaving duty are changing and watching Bregman and me hammer it out. I know the room is divided about fifty-fifty over who's right and who's wrong. It's the same unfortunate allegiances: primarily the younger fellows against the vets. Why does it have to be like this?

"You young guys come in here and you think you know everything," Bregman continues, pulling his shield off his shirt and clipping it into a leather case. He yanks off his tie. "Just remember. This was a top-flight outfit before any of you got out of diapers and into the Academy. You don't make the

166

outfit work. You're not essential. And you're not going to make any change in this fucking city. It's the same shit day to day. You do what you can and what you can't do you don't try. Figure it out, Fox. When you're older, maybe you'll be smarter also!" I catch a few smirks of agreement around the room.

I storm into the captain's office. The captain is an island of composure. He is sitting at his desk, perusing some reports from headquarters. He cannot help having overheard everything.

"I just got one request," I say to him. "I don't work with Bregman again. Any other partner in the place! But not this guy!"

The cap never looks up. "Sounds like a good idea," he says. And that's all he says. I stand there a second waiting for more. Then I go back to the locker room where everyone avoids my eye. Slowly I calm down.

Sheppard appears near my locker, already changed to go home. "What's buggin' you, Billy?" he asks.

I look at him. "You heard everything." I motion toward Bregman and some of the others. "That's what's bothering me."

He shakes his head and lights one of his cancerous cigarettes. "No," he says. "That's not what I mean. What's *really* bothering you?"

Fifteen

I am sitting at a large wooden table covered with magazines. I am in a dayroom of the psychiatric ward at Bellevue. I am waiting for Michael who I have not seen for fourteen days, since before they put him in isolation. We have not spoken, either.

I am nervous but don't know why. Patients wander around the room. Some are so sadly detached from reality that I look away. One comes up to me and starts talking about the colors of flowers and wanders off again.

Then a door opens at the far end of the room and I see Michael. It is jarring to recognize someone in these surroundings.

He gives me a big grin as he approaches, half boy, half young man, sheepish to be here and pleased to be the center of someone's attention.

"How you doing, guy?" I ask as he comes to the table.

"Hi, Bill."

I give him a firm handshake and a slight hug on the shoulders. "You look better. They feeding you okay?" I ask.

"Yeah. I'm eating okay."

"How about these doctors? They doing right by you?"

"Yeah. They're okay, too."

"How about the nurses? I'll bet you got a favorite."

He gives me a sly grin. "Yeah, there's this blonde who's kinda cute," he admits. "Her name's Barbara. I talk to her a lot."

We exchange some more small talk. Then I reach for the bandages at his wrists. "Tell me about this," I say to him. "I heard a story I didn't like."

With a pained expression he tries to move the wrists away. "I done something stupid," he admits. "You know."

"What did you use?"

"I sharpened a plastic knife from lunch."

He removes the soiled bandages from his wrists. I hold up his palm and look at the long dark scars. "What'd you do that for? I told you you were going to get help."

He shrugs and pulls his hand away. "I got discouraged, I guess."

"Why?"

"Nobody came to see me. I figured you were just bullshitting me. I figured I was forgotten about again. So what was the use?"

"Michael, didn't they tell you? They were holding you in isolation. I tried to get in to see you, but they wouldn't let me through."

"Yeah," he says, "I know that now. They told me two days ago."

I grimace and wonder how many years it will take him to fully trust another human being, if ever.

169

"Mike," I say. "I don't make promises just to hear myself talk. I promised I was going to help you. Whatever problem you have, whatever happens, you can always count on me. Do you understand?"

He nods slowly. "Yeah."

"Then put that on file. And remember it."

"Yeah," he says again. Then he looks up. "What about the other promises?" he asks. "The ones up on the roof. The room in your house."

"It's there."

"How about school? I want to go back to school."

"Mike, this is a big one and you're going to have to be patient. I'm working on everything I promised you. But I got to deal with people in these state agencies."

His expression falls. "I know all about state agencies," he says dejectedly. "They been shuffling me around since I was nine."

"You're in New York now, Mike. This is different."

"I want to get out of here. I don't like being locked up."

"There's a nice couple from the suburbs who are interested in you, too." I tell him, trying to rally his spirits. "They're nice people. They have a nice home."

"I met them earlier today," he says. "Dr. Farber introduced me."

"What'd you think?"

He shrugs. "I liked them. I don't know them, though. You, I know."

"Yeah, but Mike," I hear myself saying, "they might have a better situation for you. Ever think of that? You'd have a mother *and* a father there."

"I guess."

"You and I can always be friends and stay in touch. No matter what happens."

He looks up. "Yeah?" he asks. He thinks about it. "How 'bout if I want to ride in that van of yours someday? The R.E.P. Can I do that?"

"I promise," I tell him. "That's easy. But you've got to do something for me in return."

"What's that?"

"Be patient. You've got a lot of people outside this hospital who are trying to help you. Don't give up now." He nods. "Deal, Michael?" I ask.

"Deal," he says.

I give him a handclasp and get up to leave. It is almost three o'clock. I don't want to go running into the precinct at the last minute again.

He stands up in his loosely fitting hospital gown and institutional sneakers. Yes, he is being well cared for. But I can't shake the impersonal nature of his attire. As I leave, I catch Michael out of the corner of my eye. He waves and I wave back. He watches me go.

In the hallway outside I am thinking about his clothing. I will be at work until midnight and won't be able to do any shopping before tomorrow morning. But in the morning, I can go to the Staten Island mall. I can get him some jeans, a few sweatshirts, and some real sneakers. Maybe even a little transistor radio if I can find one that doesn't cost too much. A few possessions of his own, I think to myself, can't hurt.

I am aware of a woman's footsteps coming toward me, the distinctive click of high heels. But I am daydreaming until I hear the voice.

"Mr. Fox. Hello," she says.

I look up and recognize Ruth Blaylock, Michael's prospective foster mother.

"Oh, hello," I say to her. "Mike's got a busy day today," I joke.

171

"I'm not here to see Mike this time."

"No?" I note her subdued expression. "Anything wrong?" I ask.

'I'm on my way to see Dr. Farber. Maybe you should come with me."

"What about your husband?"

"He doesn't know I'm here. Please, come with me. I think this affects you, also."

I glance at my watch. At worst I'll call the precinct and explain everything. So they may dock me. That's life.

Moments later I am sitting in Dr. Farber's office and Ruth Blaylock is talking. She is composed and speaks resolutely, but her words do not come easily.

Her husband was married once before, she tells me, and he had a son. The marriage ended in divorce in 1976. But two years before the divorce, she goes on in a brave voice, her husband and his son were on a boating trip off the coast of Florida. Both father and son misread the brightening horizon. Their boat overturned in a squall. The father managed to cling to the boat. The son did not, though he did wear a life preserver. In the waves father and son became separated. When the boy was found, he was suffering from exposure. The doctors were unable to save him.

"My husband's son would be just about Michael's age today," she concludes. "And I know that's what my husband is seeking to recapture." She shakes her head. "My husband is fifty-five," she concludes. "I know Mike is a troubled boy. We'd love to have him in our home. But," she hesitates, then goes on. "But Mike has run away from so many other homes. Do you know what it would do to my husband if Mike rejected him. In six months? In a year? I think it would kill him."

Dr. Farber blows a long stream of smoke from his pipe. He glances at me and then looks back to Mrs. Blaylock.

"I can understand," he says.

"George mustn't ever learn that I came here and told you this," she says. "I'm sorry. Mike isn't the son for us."

There is a heavy silence in the room. Then Dr. Farber turns to me.

"I guess we might make a father out of you after all, Mr. Fox."

"We've got to contend with Health and Hospitals first," I answer. "Michael says they want to move him out of here in a couple of days. To Spofford," I add.

"There's a way around that," he says softly, relighting his pipe. I listen. "If you want to pursue adoption—"

"I do."

"—we can ask Michael to voluntarily commit himself to the psychiatric ward. That way he can stay here for—" Dr. Farber glances at a desktop calendar, "for another two weeks. Until early October."

I start to grin. Sure enough. A small quirk in the system. Now if only we can find a larger one.

"It's all up to Michael, of course," Dr. Farber concludes. "He has to commit himself. He has to sign a paper."

"When can you ask him?"

"Today. Why are you smiling, Mr. Fox?"

"He'll sign."

"You seem certain." Dr. Farber is starting to smile, also.

"I am certain," I answer. "You see, I'm getting to know Michael pretty well."

That same afternoon, Michael commits himself to Bellevue Psychiatric. We have won a small victory and have bought ourselves two weeks. I see Michael next day and present him with some new clothes.

*   *   *

The odds are still against us. I am a single male parent and Child Placement is throwing every obstacle in my way. The days tick by. Michael cannot commit himself a second time to buy two more weeks. We have played our only trump card.

I do not feel that I am a full-time cop anymore. I go to work. I do my job. But my mind is often elsewhere. The captain and sergeants keep me away from certain partners. I work mostly with Gary, sometimes with Shep or Paul. We have a river rescue. We have a pair of construction accidents. We have a car crash in the East Village that wipes out a family. I work with my Scout Troop one night a week and with the Explorers' Post on Saturdays. I am tired. I see Michael as often as I can.

"How long am I going to stay in here?" he asks me. It is everything I can do to keep him patient. I feel like going over to Child Placement and cracking heads together to shake out the cobwebs.

I go to see Michael one morning and do a doubletake. There is polish on his fingernails.

"What the hell's this?" I ask, grabbing his hand.

Then he tells me. I cannot believe my ears.

The Blaylocks had been screened carefully before being allowed to see Mike. So had I. But yesterday, out of the blue, a man calling himself Mr. Summers arrived at Bellevue. He says he is from the Police Athletic League and is admitted to see Mike.

I learn that Summers smells like a kept woman and wears an earring. He is not exactly what the P.A.L. sends around but somehow, this doesn't bother anyone.

He has told Mike that he will soon be adopting him instead of me, that he will put him on health food and pills to help cure his depression. Then he pulls out some nail polish and

174

wanted to do Mike's fingers. Three and a half fingers and Mike took off toward the private rooms.

"Jesus H. Christ!" I explode. I go storming over to Dr. Farber's office. Dr. Farber knows nothing about it. "Security around here," he says, "can be a little exasperating sometimes."

But now I am steaming. Summers turns up again the next day and Mike calls me. I leave work, citing a family emergency, and fly over to Bellevue. Mr. Summers has left by the time I get there and Michael is in a frenzy. He is every bit as agitated as the night I took him off the roof.

"That guy's going to get me," Michael cries as I hold him. "I know he's going to get me. They always get me."

"Who does? Who?"

"Queers!" he screams. "Tennessee. North Carolina. Ohio. San Francisco. They're always after me!"

He sobs in terror. He tells me stories about certain institutions that he had never mentioned before. I try to calm him and reason with him.

"I'm making you another promise, Michael," I tell the trembling boy. "As long as I'm alive, none of these guys will lay a hand on you. I'll break their skulls open first. Goddamn it, I mean it!"

"You got to get me out of here," he cries.

"You're right. I do."

Michael is calmer but I am not. I go directly to Child Placement. I am tired of being polite and civil with people who appear to be working against Michael's interests.

I ask for an immediate appointment with the supervisor I once spoke to on the telephone. I want the next steps of the adoptive procedure to be taken immediately. I tell him that I am not leaving his office until he schedules me for the in-home screening interview.

175

"Friday of next week," he finally allows.

"Tomorrow," I say.

"Impossible."

I settle into a chair in his office as if preparing for a long sit.

"All right," he says with great irritation a few minutes later. "I'll send an investigator to your house tomorrow morning."

"Much better," I tell him.

A woman arrives the next morning. I introduce her to my mother and I show her the room Michael will have. Mother serves her some coffee and she asks me many questions, some of them quite pointed and suggestive.

Why, she wants to know, am I not married? Was I ever interested in girls? What exactly do I expect to get out of this? Money? Publicity?

I tell her about Mary Beth and Kathlene. I mention Tina. I tell her about modern women, careers, and my idea of a proper home. I can tell this woman doesn't like me.

Yet I pass her scrutiny and am sent to a psychiatrist employed by the Child Placement Service. I have not been to a psychiatrist since my pre-induction examination into the police department. He asks me more questions, many of them centering around my parents and sex life. I wonder how anyone gets through these procedures.

One by one, the days disappear from the calendar. I have finished running the Child Placement guantlet and Mike has only three days left at Bellevue. I speak again to the supervisor of his case and learn that I have done well on my examinations.

"Great," I answer. "When can Michael move over here?"

"You did well," he tells me. "But that doesn't mean you get custody."

"Then what the hell does it mean?"

176

It means that Child Placement will consider my application for several weeks. Maybe a few months. Then they will let me know.

Christ Almighty. I am back where I started.

I talk to Helen Mayron again. "See what I mean?" she answers sadly. "These people are impossible."

I call Dr. Farber. We commiserate. "I'm at my wit's end on this, myself," he says. "I wish I could think of something. Everything takes so damned much time."

"Time is the enemy," I agree. "Time and red tape."

I am at home on the next to the last day of September. It is evening. My sister and her husband are visiting with her kids.

The telephone rings. I pick it up and recognize Tina's voice. I have been neglecting her. "Still talking to me?" I tease.

"I'm talking to a lot of people," she answers, "for this crazy cop I know."

"How do you mean?" I ask.

"I ran into an old friend yesterday," Tina tells me. "A girl I went to school with. She works for a child welfare agency."

"Don't tell me about it," I moan.

"She knows all about you and Michael," Tina continues. "And she knows how you can beat the system."

My ears perk up. "She knows what?" I ask.

"She told me something very unofficial," Tina says. "So you can't reveal how you found out. You have to keep it hush-hush."

"I'm an expert at keeping secrets," I tell her. "Quick before I faint, tell me what to do."

"Don't try to adopt Michael," says Tina.

I draw a breath. "Look," I tell her, "I like the boy. I want

177

to help him. I want to bring him into our family. No one's going to change my decision to—"

"That's not what I mean," she says. "My friend has seen dozens of cases like this. There's only one way to beat the adoption system."

My mood changes. "I'm listening," I tell her.

"Where are Michael's parents?"

"Mike tells me his mother's probably dead. His father lives out West."

"Does his father want him?"

I laugh. "I doubt it," I tell her.

"When will Michael be eighteen? Six months, right?"

"Right."

She speaks clearly and concisely. "Drop the adoption proceedings. File instead for temporary legal custody. The court will probably award it to you since the State of New York doesn't want Michael, either. You can probably get Michael released from Bellevue directly to you."

"But for how long?" I ask. "And then what?"

"Then you file for permanent legal custody. If no one challenges, Michael will be able to stay with you for months. By that time he'll be of legal age. No one will be able to touch him."

As I put down the telephone, I am struck dumb by the simple revelation. I think back to Helen Mayron. Yes, indeed, the system has a quirk to it.

"What was that?" my sister asks.

I am grinning like the Cheshire Cat. "Tina. With the miracle we've been waiting for," I tell her. "Come on. Get your coat."

"What's going on?" my mother asks.

We are off to see a friend who is a lawyer. I want him working on custody papers that night.

The next day I see Michael again. I can barely control my excitement. But all I tell him is to be patient, perhaps for as little as one more day.

"They're going to ship me to Spofford any hour now," he says morosely. "I know it. I can feel it."

"Hang in, Michael," I beg. "We're fighting for you."

Then we are in Family Court on Staten Island. I am accompanied by Michael's social worker, Helen Mayron, and his psychiatrist, Dr. Eugene Farber. We go before the judge and I present papers asking the court's permission to be granted temporary legal custody of Michael Buchanan, now residing in Bellevue Hospital.

The judge looks at the motion. "Who are you, Mr. Fox?" he asks, studying the application.

"I'm the police officer who took the boy off the rooftop, Your Honor," I tell him.

He looks up from the application and peers down from his bench at me. He reminds me of a desk sergeant. But then he breaks into a smile and says, "Why, yes. So you are." Everyone in the world, it seems, watches the six o'clock news.

Dr. Farber reports on Michael's present condition. Helen Mayron speaks in favor of letting Michael move into my home. The judge asks me if I have any experience with adoptive children.

I tell him about the youth groups I've worked with. I mention that my brother Jimmy, who has five natural children, has also brought an adoptive son into the family.

"How is it working out?" the judge asks.

"Very well, sir," I tell him.

Suddenly it is all so simple. The judge will place Michael in my custody under three conditions. I must make an effort to locate his natural parents. I must enroll him in school. And

I must return on a pre-arranged date in November, the day after Thanksgiving as it happens, for a second custody hearing. His stipulations are wise and reasonable.

Then he grants me the court's permission to take custody of Michael as a foster son. Not since joining the police department has there been a prouder moment in my life. From Dr. Farber, I obtain Michael's discharge papers from Bellevue.

I drive to Manhattan. I am under no illusions that the future will be easy. I have never been a parent before; Michael has a lot of growing up to do and a lot of problems to sort out. But together we can both learn and grow. Within me is the joyous feeling that springs from a loving commitment to another human being.

I park my car near the hospital, walk to Michael's ward, and ask to see him. An orderly goes to find him as I wait in the day room.

I watch the other patients and feel a surge of compassion for all of them. I am lost in this thought when I hear Michael's voice.

"Hey, Bill," he says to me. "What's going on? What are you doing here again?"

I hand him several huge shopping bags that I've carried from my car, and he looks at me in total astonishment.

"Go pack up your things, son," I tell him. "We're going home."

Sixteen

"DON'T delude yourself for a moment," Dr. Farber warned me. "You're going to be sorely tested when things get difficult for Mike. He has stolen cars. He's been a professional shoplifter. He has stowed away on airplanes. He even set fire to a house when he didn't feel secure with a particular family. You shouldn't leave him at home alone."

"Well, if Mike's had some tough times, so have I," I told the doctor. "Maybe we're ideally suited to each other."

"I've thought of that, too," he answered. "In many ways, I agree. A strong male figure might be of more use to him than a family unit."

Then he gave me the name of a psychiatrist on Staten Island with whom Michael is to continue. But Michael and I are not thinking about doctors as we walk from Bellevue to my car. We are thinking how quickly everything has happened. A month ago Michael was friendless and alone; I was a bachelor.

Now Michael is coming into a family. And I have a seventeen-year-old son.

As we climb into my car, suddenly he asks me, "Hey? Where is Staten Island, anyway?" We both break up in laughter.

"Don't worry, Mike," I tell him. "Half the people in Manhattan don't know where it is, either."

We drive across the Brooklyn Bridge, with Michael watching as the view of Manhattan unfurls and widens behind us. We drive past the warehouse and pier districts of Brooklyn and then across the vast roadway of the Verrazano. (And, yes, both times I look up toward the heights of the bridges as I drive.) Then we are in Staten Island—and home.

As Michael and I enter the house, my mother beams, happy as she always is with any new addition to the family. She now has an even dozen grandchildren.

Michael's room is a nine-by-twelve-foot area on the first floor of the house, just off the den where the television, the electric organ, and the Atari setup are kept. "It's not luxurious, Mike," I tell him. "But it's yours." Michael walks in with the wide eyes of an expectant child, looking the walls up and down, peering out the window and searching in the closet.

My mother appears with some clothes we've bought for him. He thanks her very formally. But he is transfixed with his room.

"What was here last?" he asks.

"Well," I tell him with a shrug, "it's just been an extra room for a number of years. Before that, when my brothers and sisters were growing up, my parents had this room. Our rooms were upstairs."

"It's great," he says excitedly. Then he curls his lower lip inquisitively and a slight frown crosses his face.

"Hey, Bill," he says, "you don't mind if I put some posters up, do you?"

I laugh. "Make yourself at home, Mike, 'cause that's where you are."

Later my brothers stop by to meet the new arrival. So does Eileen and her husband. Then, toward evening, I call my partner, Gary.

"Hey, guess who's here at the house," I ask him.

"Who?"

"Mike."

There is silence. "Mike who?" he runs through the names of other cops. "Mike Stapleton? Mike McGrory? Mike O'Connell?"

"Nope," I tell him. "Mike from the roof."

"Oh. That Mike." There is a pause and then he almost shouts into the telephone: "What's *he* doing at your house?"

I want more than anything to give Michael a normal home and a chance to move to adulthood like any teenager. I enroll him at Curtis High School and he is placed in the eleventh grade. He starts his classes and seems to handle them well.

I give him an NYPD T-shirt that he wears proudly around the house. And I look into his room one day to see that the posters have indeed gone up—Loni Anderson, Bo Derek, and the New York Yankees.

Then it happens. A reporter from the Staten Island *Advance,* a man who saw me at the courthouse during our custody hearing, calls me. "I have a story here that I can't believe," he says. "You adopted this boy you rescued from the roof?"

"I didn't adopt him," I say. "I was granted temporary legal custody."

"So the boy is in your house living with you?"

183

"That's correct."

"Why?"

"I made promises to him. And someone had to step in to help. I can't sit around and know a life is being wasted when I could have helped."

Within an hour twelve more reporters call. When I take the telephone off the hook, they appear at the door. I honestly cannot believe it.

The next day there are fifty reporters and the whole thing is out of control.

"Mike," I say, "we've got to make a decision. We can tell these people that it's a private matter. Or we can open the doors, talk to them, and see what happens."

Michael thinks for only a moment. "Let's talk," he says.

"I knew you'd say that," I grin. So we open he doors. The next thing I know I'm getting offers from movie producers who want to get me the best table at Elaine's and have me squired around town in a limousine.

This is followed by an avalanche of mail. It comes to my home and to the precinct. Over the next few weeks I receive more than eleven hundred letters from people I have never met and who want to help. They say they are praying for us and send us their words of encouragement. Some include money, which goes into the trust fund Gary and I opened for Mike through the P.B.A.

One letter comes from Washington, D.C. It is addressed to me and Michael. Like the others, it is a note of encouragement and good will. It is signed by President Ronald Reagan.

"Wow," says Michael.

I shake my head in wonder. "Yeah," I agree. "Wow." Five weeks ago, nobody cared whether Michael Buchanan lived or died. Now he is receiving mail from the President of the United

States. He is the same boy and I am the same cop. And there must be at least another sixty thousand kids out on the streets while Michael is receiving this tidal wave of attention. I pray that our story may lead to changes for a few of them.

"I'll tell you exactly what's going to happen," says Tommy McCarthy as he sits at the Gray Table. "That punk kid is going to steal stuff out of Fox's house and take off with it."

There are nods of agreement. The cynicism runs deep at the Gray Table, a product of men who have seen too much in this city and forgotten none of it. My taking custody of Michael has put a spotlight on the Emergency Squad. Some of the veterans are resentful. If anyone should be getting headlines, they growl, it should be men who have been on the job for ten and fifteen years. I have been there for ten months.

"Or you know what else?" adds Joe Bregman. "The kid'll grab his off-duty revolver one night and blow away somebody."

"Maybe he'll blow Fox away," McCarthy mutters.

"Hey, Billy's not a bad buy," Gary interjects. "You guys just don't understand."

"What's there to understand?" Bregman asks. "He's out to be a hero. He's out for the personal headlines."

"He's trying to help a kid," Shep says.

"We all try to help kids," bitches another vet. "But you don't have to go coddling punks that bring out thirty cops to the Bowery for a whole shift. Jesus Christ. Why waste your time?"

Paulie Redecha is studying for his B.S. and takes time to look up from his ever-present textbook long enough to chip in his opinion. "I met the kid," he says.

"And what'd you think? A punk, right?" McCarthy asks.

185

"Nice kid. Deserves a break," Paulie says. Then he lowers his gaze and disappears back into his book.

"Ah, what do you know, Redecha?" asks McCarthy.

The department has given me this day off to tend to some personal matters regarding Michael's custody.

"If they got something to say to me," I tell Gary the next day, "they can say it to my face. But maybe they don't have the balls for that."

Moments later I am at my locker. On it there is a clipping about a sergeant in the NYPD who has recently come out of the closet and revealed that he is gay, a move of conscience and infinite courage. There is a picture of the sergeant. Next to it is taped my picture, torn from the New York *Post*.

"First a sergeant, now an E-Man," someone has scribbled. I stifle my anger. I smile. And I crumple the clipping and toss it into the wastebasket. People with minds such as these are worth nothing more.

Michael tests me, also. He tests me as a father, as a big brother, and as an authority figure. He tests me in ways I could never have imagined.

We are playing Atari Missile Command. When he begins to lose, he accidentally hits the "re-start" button, erasing the game and the score.

He is playing the organ at seven o'clock. I remind him of his homework. Ten minutes later he is still playing. I walk past the organ and turn it off. I remain there with my finger pressed on the OFF button. I say nothing further.

"I guess it's time for homework," he says.

He is the same as any other teenager with the telephone. He has friends, both male and female, at high school. He talks to them endlessly. Homework time, I remind him. Again, he resists. One night he tests me until I walk to the telephone, remove it from his hand, and hang it up.

186

Michael explodes. "You have no right to do that!" he says. "You insulted my friends!"

"I warned you, Mike," I tell him calmly. "There are rules in this house. You don't set them. I do."

"You got no right!" he screams. He storms from my den upstairs. He goes down the steps and I wait anxiously to hear which door slams. I hear it. It's the door to his room and not the front door. I smile to myself and breathe a sigh of relief. I have won a small battle.

There are no hard feelings. Michael sulks in his room for an hour, finishes his homework, and pops his head out. "How about a round of Missile Command?" he asks.

"You finish your homework, guy?"

"Yup."

"You going to cheat me this time," I gibe him. "Or are you going to try to beat me fair and square for a change?"

"Cheat?" he asks with an ear-to-ear grin. "I never cheat at Missile Command."

Out comes the Atari and our living room is filled with bleeps, sonar pulses, and electronic explosions. Mike is now beating me fair and square.

But if I am tested, so is Michael. Each morning I give him lunch money as he leaves for school. The initial reports I get from his teachers are good. Mike's no slouch in the classroom. He joins the school newspaper, the bowling team, and sings with a choral group. Everything is fine . . . or so I think.

Then one day in October I get a truancy report. Michael has received a failing grade in math. He has not been going to math class.

"Hey," I say to him that night after dinner, "what's this all about? You haven't been going to a class."

He is surprised I know. "How did you find out?"

"What do you mean, how did I find out? You don't think they contact a parent if a boy doesn't show for a class?"

"I'm not doing well in the class," he begins.

"So you thought you'd skip a few days?"

He doesn't say anything, but his expression tells me the real answer.

"I thought you wanted a diploma," I say. "I thought this was important to you."

"It is, but—"

"So how are you going to get a diploma without math?"

"I don't know."

"Mike, one thing you're going to have to learn is that you don't solve your problems by running away from them."

"Yeah," he shrugs.

"Do you have problems in the class? Is somebody giving you a hard time?"

"No," he says sullenly. "It's all right. I'll start going again."

I can't explain why I am unconvinced. I call his math teacher and discover the difficulty. In one class Michael came up with a foolish answer to a question. The whole class exploded with laughter. Michael lost his composure and began screaming.

"Uh oh!" one of the boys taunted. "We better lay off him or he'll go up to the roof and threaten to jump."

With this, Michael flew into an even greater rage, turned over his desk and chair and fled the classroom. The teacher brought him back but Michael has been frequently absent ever since.

I sit down with Michael again. "There's only one way to stick it to people when they give you a hard time like that, Mike," I tell him. "And that's to show them how insignificant they are."

"Bill, some of these guys have been on me every day I've been there."

"Yeah, Mike," I tell him. "I'm sure they have. And the next place you go someone's going to be trying to kick your ass for something else. There's always something and there's always someone."

"So what do I do?"

"You know what you do, Mike? You go into class better prepared than they are. You ignore anything they say to you and you show them up by being better than they are. They're not going to like it. But maybe then they'll start to feel a little uneasy in that class."

He nods. He goes to math. His grades in the course rise not quite to a B, but at least above passing.

Some things prove more difficult. The problem of Michael's parents looms. Our next custody hearing is fast approaching. I can tell that the tension is mounting in Michael. He has learned that court hearings are tools to shuttle him from one institution to the next. He dreads them.

As the date approaches, he wakes one morning to find that he has wet his bed. He tries to hide it. But it's not the type of thing that hides easily.

"Hey, Mike," I say. "Looks like you had a little trouble here."

He hangs his head. I know what the psychiatrist once told me. In one home Michael was expelled for bedwetting. At another, he was beaten.

"I'll make you a bet, Mike," I tell him. "I'll bet there isn't a guy in this country who hasn't had the same problem at least a couple of times."

He looks at me strangely. "Yeah?"

"The worst part," I tell him, "is that it makes you so nervous you're afraid you'll do it again."

He smiles sheepishly. "Yeah, I know."

189

"I'll tell you what: you worry about your school work and I'll worry about everything else."

"What about my parents?" he asks.

"I'll worry about them, too."

Yet Michael continues to worry about his parents. And the concern springs from deep inside. It is a phobia and a fixation, and it is a wound that will not heal.

One night in late October, Gary and I collar a robbery suspect a block from our precinct. We stay late to turn the man over to an anti-crime unit so he can be processed for booking.

I do not get home until 2 A.M. Just as I am preparing for bed, I hear Michael in his bedroom crying.

I knock on his door and push it open. "What's wrong?"

"Aw, Bill," he says, sitting up in his bed, "you don't understand this one."

I turn on the light and sit down on the edge of his bed. "Try me."

"My mother," he says.

"What about her?"

He shakes his head and the tears flow freely. "Do you know what it's like growing up never knowing?" he says. "I don't know who she is. I don't know what she looks like. I don't know anything about her."

"I know, Mike," I tell him. "That's a rough one to live with.

All my life I've wondered. I've wanted to know. Everyone else has a mother," he sobs. "Why don't I?"

This time he has me. I really don't know what to say. I am trained in my job to react instinctively and to come up with answers. Here, early in the morning in my own home, Michael has caught me unprepared. I can only respond with the truth.

"Mike, we're trying to find her," I tell him. "We're doing everything. Last known address, relatives."

"But you can't find her? And we can't find my old man, either?"

"His last address was the motel in Memphis."

"Maybe they're both dead," he suggests. "Maybe I'll never know."

I put my arm around his shoulders. I can almost feel his fears and insecurities and the questions that torment him.

"Mike, you're looking at it the wrong way," I tell him. "You're looking at it backwards."

"I want to know who she was," he insists.

"Of course you do. And we'll find out. I promise you. But you have to look ahead, not back. The important thing is your future. It's okay to think about your mother from time to time. It's natural to wonder. But you must look forward, not back."

"Yeah, Bill, I know," he says. "But it isn't easy."

"Mike," I say, "nothing that's important in life is easy. It's the difficult things that force you to be a man. You're just realizing that now. That's what's so painful."

"I guess," he says.

It is a scene and a subject that arises from one day to the next, in one form or another. The identity of Michael's parents, particularly his mother, is a question that will not go away.

Mike and I discuss it at length. Mike and his psychiatrist approach the problem regularly. To Michael, rootless for so long, it is most important. And, meanwhile, the date for our hearing on permanent legal custody approaches too quickly. I make phone calls to three states and have child welfare bureaus in those three states working on it for me. Without a death certificate for his parents, or without their consent, I will never gain full custody of my son. And he, of course, will remain

191

in the legal and psychological limbo that tortures him in the early morning hours.

Then everything happens at once.

I pick up the telephone and hear the voice of a reporter from Associated Press who has been covering the case.

"I've got something for you," he says.

"Do I want it?" I say.

"Probably. It's Michael's father's telephone number."

I bolt to attention. "Where'd you get that?" I ask.

"I got it from the father himself," the reporter tells me. "The father telephoned our bureau in Las Vegas. He's planning to sue you."

"Sue me? For what?"

"Libel. Slander. Anything else he can think of."

"Why?"

"He claims he never abused the boy and that you're telling lies about him to the press."

"Better let me have the telephone number," I say. The reporter dictates it and I write it down on the note pad near the telephone.

I look at the calendar. We have three weeks left before our next custody hearing. I wonder if Mike's father is bent on making trouble, getting his son back, or just clearing his name.

There is only one way to find out. I dial the Nevada exchange.

A Southern-inflected man's voice answers, "Hello?"

I draw a breath, then speak. "My name is William Fox. I'm a police officer in New York City and I'd like to speak with the father of Michael Buchanan."

There is a pause on the line.

"What that boy is saying about me is lies," I am told. The voice is astonishing—it sounds so much like Michael's. "I

192

never abused the kid," the man says, and he begins a long disclaimer of everything that Michael has said publicly.

"I didn't leave him in the car for long at the carnival. And I never beat him."

Michael's father tells me about Michael's childhood and the youngster's severe emotional problems after his grandparents died.

"I was out on my own then," he says. "I was having a tough time. I was back from the war and I done a little drinking."

"A few girlfriends here and there, too?" I ask.

"Look," he counters, "I'm remarried now. I got a back injury and my wife has to work. I got a little girl. We try to live peacefully."

"I'm trying to reach his mother, also. Do you know where she is?" I ask.

After a hesitation, Mike's father says that he ran into his ex-wife in Tennessee three years earlier.

"She says she's got another son of mine," he adds. "But I don't know. She wouldn't let me see him."

"Michael has a full brother?" I ask.

"That's what she says, Mr. Fox. But I don't know. You know what I mean?"

I am still thinking about this when he continues. "I love the boy, Mr. Fox. I don't have nothing against Michael. But I can't afford him."

I go back to what is most pressing. "I'm trying to get legal custody of Mike," I tell him. "If you want Mike down there with you—"

"No, no, I couldn't." He paused. "Do you think I could talk to him?" he asks.

"I don't know whether he wants to talk to you," I tell him. "But I'll ask."

"You ask him, Mr. Fox. I want to talk to Michael."

"What about custody?" I repeat.

"I can't do anything for the boy, Mr. Fox," he says. "I won't stand in your way. I'll sign whatever you want. I just want to talk to my son again."

After dinner that evening I sit down with Michael. I tell him I located his father. I can see the mood of apprehension that sweeps across the boy. "What'd he say?"

"He says he loves you, Mike," I said. "He wishes you well, but he can't take you in with him. He also wants to talk to you."

"My father owes me over seven thousand dollars in child support," Michael says bitterly. "It's right in the court papers from Tennessee."

"I know," I tell him. "I've seen them, too. Do you want to talk to him.?"

"No," Michael says. But two days later he changes his mind and telephones his father in Nevada. They talk for an hour. Michael says little. His father tries to mend fences. For the most part, Michael listens and mumbles an occasional "Uh huh."

"Well," I ask a visibly drained Michael when he hangs up. "What'd he say?"

"He's my own father," Michael replies quietly. "And I don't even know the man. I wouldn't even have recognized the voice."

I almost tell Michael that he and his father sound a lot alike. But I catch myself in time and say nothing.

It is half past a rainy midnight a few days later and I am tired. I have been sleeping little recently. I have had mandatory overtime at work and also have been trying to remain active with the Explorers Fire Club. And I have my obligations to Michael. As I walk up the front steps of my home, there is a quick movement on the porch.

For a moment there is a flash of fear within me as an entire other world returns—the world I knew while working undercover for the F.B.I. There are people in this city who would like to settle a few grudges, and they might well do it on a dark night in the shadows of my front porch.

Instinctively I reach toward my ankle where my off-duty revolver is holstered. But then I hear an adolescent voice.

"Mr. Fox?"

I freeze and look closely. A boy steps from the far end of the porch. He is cold and wet and shivering. I recognize him as one of the boys in my former scout troop.

"Kenny, what are you doing here at this hour?"

"I ran away from home," he says. "You got to help me."

The rain is starting up again. I look at him and only begin to understand. "Come inside," I tell him.

I unlock the door.

Michael peeks out of his room and then goes back to sleep. I sit down with Kenny in the living room. When I give him a glass of milk, the boy starts crying. I can barely understand him, but I already know the problem. I know Kenny. I know his home. His mother is rarely home as she spends more time on her social life than on her family. Kenny doesn't have a father.

"When did you run away?" I ask.

He shrugs his shoulders. I press and he tells me. He has been on the streets for a week. He has not been going to school and he has scarcely eaten. He wants to stay here with Michael and me.

I know what I must do. I make some sandwiches and ex-

195

plain. I can't take him in and he must go back home and return to school.

"If you do that for me, I'll talk to your mother," I promise him. "You've got obligations. One of them is your education. But she's got obligations, too. And her family should come before her social life."

"You'll tell her that?" Kenny asks.

"I'll tell her that."

"What if she says it's none of your business?"

"I'll tell her she's not completely right. I'm a police officer, too, you know. If a minor is on the street unattended, it becomes my business."

Kenny stays a while longer. Then I call his mother. I tell her that I'm getting in the car with him and bringing him home.

"Oh," she says sleepily, "he's been with you. I been wondering."

Later in the week I will talk to her. But not now. Returning home, I see the letter I was carrying when I met Kenny.

I sit down and read it. It is from a woman in Texas who has seen Michael and me on her local television news. She says she is Michael's grandmother. And she has enclosed the name and address of a woman living outside of Ft. Worth.

The woman is her daughter. And her daughter, she says, is Michael's mother.

The number I have dialed is ringing and a female voice answers. I ask for the woman by name.

"This is her," she says.

"I'm Police Officer Fox and I'm calling from New York. Are you the mother of Michael Buchanan?"

Before the woman can even speak, she begins to cry. It is obvious that she is Michael's mother.

"I thought he was dead," she tells me after regaining control of her voice. "His father told me he was dead in a motorcycle accident."

"No, ma'am," I tell her. "He's alive. I have him with me."

Again, she cries but continues to talk. She begins her own account of Michael's past, an account that intersects only occasionally with that of Michael's father.

"Where *is* his father?" she asks. "He owes me alimony."

"I'm only concerned with Michael," I answer. "He's under psychiatric care, but otherwise he's healthy. I have him in school here in New York."

"What will happen to him?" she asks.

I tell her that he will stay with me if no other custody is arranged. If she wants him back and if he wishes to go, I will send him home, I tell her. But there she stops me.

"Are you doing well with him?" she asks. "Do you and Michael get on okay together?"

"Very well," I tell her.

She speaks in a tired, drained voice. "You might do best by him," she says. "I got two other boys. I don't have extra room or extra money. I work as a waitress and my husband works and it's all we can do just to pay our bills."

"I understand," I tell her.

"Will he talk to me?"

"I don't know. I'd have to ask him."

"You got to understand," she says. "I love my son. But I don't know who he is. I haven't seen him for sixteen years."

I tell her that I wish to file for permanent legal custody. I explain the court procedures and inform her that she's free to contact me or change her mind. She tells me that she understands.

"You do what's best for the boy," she says.

"The papers that are being sent down," I explain, "will attest to the fact that I spoke to you about Michael. If you wish to challenge my custody hearing, you'll have to be in court in Staten Island the day after Thanksgiving."

"Are you sure you can't tell me where my husband is?" she asks again. "Do you know how many years of alimony he owes me?"

That afternoon, I tell Michael that I have spoken to his mother. His face goes cold and freezes with the tension. He wants to know every word that we said to each other. He makes me go over and over the conversation I had with the woman whom he has never known and about the brothers whom he never knew existed.

"She says she thought you were dead," I tell him.

"She didn't look for me very hard," he says. "She could have kept looking until she found a grave. Couldn't she, Bill?"

"I can't answer for her, Mike. She says she loves you."

"Why didn't she come forward herself? Why did my grandmother have to write to you?"

"I don't know, Michael. Maybe she's afraid of your reaction. Maybe she feels that since she can't provide for you—"

Michael springs up from the sofa and paces the floor. "I'm not talking to her!" he yells, his eyes getting red and angry. "I don't want to know about that woman. She's never cared nothing for me!"

"Michael, calm down," I say gently. "Nothing has changed for you in this house."

"Let *her* call *me!* If she calls me, maybe I'll talk. But I'm not calling her! I'll die first!"

"Okay, Mike," I say, reaching toward him to calm him down. "It's okay. You're here with me and that's where you're staying.

That's your room over there and anyone who wants to take you out of it has to fight me first."

He sits down again and draws a deep breath. He reaches for his cigarettes and nervously lights one.

"What happens next?" he asks.

"I'll call her back and tell her you don't want to talk to her."

"Good!"

"Then I send her the custody papers. She said she'd sign them."

"What about Tennessee? North Carolina? Can they take me back?"

"They can't and they won't."

"I want to know who's going to take me out of here," he says, his voice edgy. "I always get taken out. I want to know who it's going to be this time."

"It's not going to be anyone, Mike," I tell him. "You'll be able to stay here for as long as you want. Go back to what I promised you on the roof, Michael. Everything still stands."

He snuffs out the cigarette. "Something always goes wrong," he says. "I won't believe none of this till we get past the court hearing."

"Mike, even if someone tries something, you and I will fight them. Together. We can fight anyone for the six months it takes until you're eighteen. After that, no one can touch you. You're your own man then."

He blows out a long breath. "Six months," he says. "I don't think I ever been anywhere for as long as six months."

Michael's parents sign the separate set of custody papers that are served them. The papers are returned to Staten Island Family Court.

The twenty-sixth of November looms before us, and I know that deep in his heart Michael cannot believe that something will not go wrong on or before that date.

There is a knot of reporters around the entrance to the Staten Island Family Court when Michael and I arrive. I can tell how anxious Michael is, but he waves gamely to the reporters, some of whom we know well now. Then we enter the courthouse.

We are the first case on the calendar this morning. We complete some court papers and enter the judge's chambers with our attorney and an attorney for Child Placement. It is a few minutes past nine.

Like most court hearings, the difficult work—the research, the motions, the filing of information—has been done in advance. When we are all seated the judge opens a folder on his desk and withdraws the letter that contains his decision in our case.

"Michael," he says before reading the letter, "I hope you realize that few people in this world get second chances. I hope you make the best of yours."

"Yes, sir," Michael replies.

"You're a very fortunate young man to have found a home so willing to open to you," the judge continues.

"Yes, sir. I know," Michael says.

I look at Michael and I give him a smile. It helps reduce the tension and he smiles back. I can see his hands fidgeting.

The judge then rules in the case of Michael Buchanan. It is the opinion of the court, he reads from the letter, that it would be in the best interest of Michael to be awarded to the permanent legal custody of William Patrick Fox. No challenge has been received by the court from Michael's natural parents. No reason has been found by the court that such custody should not be awarded.

After reading the ruling the judge looks up. "Michael," he asks, "do you wish to stay with Mr. Fox?"

"Yes, sir. I do," Michael answers.

Then the judge turns to me. "Mr. Fox, are you willing to accept the responsibility of this boy? Education? Medical expenses?"

"Yes, sir. I am," I respond.

"So be it. Granted." The judge reaches for his seal and affixes it to the papers before him. We stand and shake hands, then the bailiff leads us downstairs. We wait in a small anteroom while the final documents are processed and sent back to the presiding judge for his signature.

A few minutes later, the court clerk hands us the executed documents. Michael breaks into a wide grin.

"That's it, kid. Too late to back out now," I tease.

We share a long handshake, and walk out to face waiting reporters. There, with as large a smile as I've ever seen from any boy, Michael reads for the press the document that makes my home his home until he is of legal age.

Seventeen

IT is December and I am tired. I am not thinking about Christmas. I am thinking about three homicides.

Three months ago in Rockland County, the bungled robbery of an armored car left two officers dead. Six terrorists from the so-called Weather Underground were arrested. One of them, Anthony LaBorde, was eventually moved to the Federal House of Detention in lower Manhattan. Another, wounded a few days later in a shootout with police near Shea Stadium (during which another officer was killed) was taken to Kings County Hospital.

Those are the three murders. And that is why I am exhausted.

The Emergency Squad in New York City is also the City's S.W.A.T. team. Although our goal is never to fire a single round, we were nonetheless the only police in New York trained in the use of heavy weapons. The intelligence division tells us that the rest of the crazies in the Weather Underground may make some attempt to free the two suspects. So every man on Emergency is spending the pre-Christmas holidays working twelve-hour shifts, from six in the morning to six in the evening. We sit, six of us at a time in each location, in the secluded wings of both the hospital and the house of detention. Six men, twenty-four hours a day, seven days a week at two different locations at a cost to the city of approximately thirty thousand dollars per week. That is the gift this Christmas from the Weather Underground to the people of New York. The tax bill, of course, will be footed by the very "working people" these self-styled revoluntionaries claim they wish to liberate.

But Michael brightens my holidays. Christmas must be viewed through the eyes of a youngster and those are just the eyes that Michael has. He is also old enough to appreciate a home and family at Christmas.

"How many cousins do I have?" he checks with me early in the month. He is writing names on a piece of paper.

"Eleven," I remind him, ranging from Jimmy's son to Eileen's son, Christopher, two.

"Two uncles and an aunt?" he continues, thinking aloud and making a list.

"Of course, two uncles and an aunt," I say. "You think I'm holding somebody out on you?"

"And one grandmother," he says aloud, drawing toward the bottom of the page. "Oh, yeah. And one father."

"Gee. Thanks."

He looks up. "This gets expensive if everyone on the list gets a gift."

"Tell me about it," I say.

"You know what? Christmas is only two weeks away. We better start our shopping early."

"Good idea, Mike." I am leafing through the evening paper. A moment later I look up and find him handing me something. "What's this?" I ask, recognizing my car keys.

"The Staten Island mall is open till eleven," he says. "Don't you think we should get a jump on gift buying?"

"Michael..."

"Please?"

So off we go gift-hunting. We return, hours later, laden with about a dozen and a half packages between us.

I work Christmas eve with Gary and it is a calm shift. Then on Christmas morning, Michael joins me and we go to early Mass. The family visits back and forth, and we exchange so many gifts that they inevitably tumble out of our arms as we go through each other's doors. That afternoon we have the big dinner at our house. Ma cooks a giant twenty-one-pound turkey and we manage to crowd the entire family around an extended table in our living room.

Michael presents me with a new cabinet to house the Atari games and the television. Where he hid it in the house so that I wouldn't find it I can't imagine. Then I watch his face light up when he opens the Konica 35-mm camera I got him. For the rest of the afternoon no one is safe from the flash of Michael's camera or from the blip-blip-blip sound of Space Invaders. It is a most happy day. In the evening Michael disappears for three hours to sing with his choral group. I relax with my brothers and sisters and we quietly marvel at how well Michael—despite the growing pains and the learning experiences we have had together—has fit into our big, bustling family.

This is how a family Christmas should be. And this is how I want them to be in the future.

* * *

Our Gang of Four on Emergency—Gary, Paulie, Shep, and I—exists no longer. Paul has transferred to the Nine Truck in Brooklyn. He is closer to his home there. He saves transportation time each day and the time he saves he can use to pursue his degree.

I am no longer working with Gary. Shep has a new partner, too. New men have moved into our unit and the veterans must train them. The new men are good. They learn quickly. Shep works with Paul Ragonese and I work with Nick Travasanti. Ragonese has come over from the Six house in Manhattan, and Travasanti was at the Central Park Precinct and got bored. Gary works with a red-haired kid named Tommy Carlyle whose father is a sergeant in the Bronx. No "sergeant jokes" around Tommy. Meanwhile, Jimmy Hatcher is gone to the Bomb Squad and Bobby Gates to the Crime Scene Unit. Richie Mueller has joined Paul Redecha at the Nine Truck and Mike McCrory has confirmed that he will definitely retire in August. The unit is in flux.

Travasanti and I are in the R.E.P. on Park Avenue South in the Twenties at a freezing 2 A.M. when a thin black woman in fish-net stockings and a blouse races toward our van. She is screaming. We look at her and see that she is not hurt, just wildly upset. We stop.

"See that fuckin' bastard over there?" she screams, pointing at a grinning man several yards in front of us. He is getting into a car with a New Jersey license. "I done something for him for fifteen dollars and he didn't pay me."

Travasanti and I blink. We look at each other. The man looks at us and waves.

We put on our overhead lights and drive a few more yards down Park Avenue and stop.

"This woman says she did something for you, guy," I say to him.

He makes a mistake. He sneers at us as he answers, "Yeah. What of it?" He is beside the open door to his car.

"She also says you didn't pay her," I continue.

We are out of the R.E.P. now, standing between the two antagonists. Nick is watching them both closely as I arbitrate.

"I *didn't* pay her," he boasts.

I look at his license plate number. "Pay her," I say to him.

"What?" he says.

"Pay her," I repeat, not batting an eyelash.

"If you owe her money for a service, you have to pay her," Nick adds with priestly sobriety.

The man stares at us as if we have lost our minds. "Do you know what she did for me?" he asks.

"No," I answer. "And I'm not interested. Unless, of course, it was illegal. In that case tell me so that we can arrest both of you."

There is a stunned silence as the man thinks about it. Then he removes fifteen dollars from his wallet and hands it to the girl.

"Now, guy," I say to him, "just for the record I'm going to write down your license number. And if I ever see you here again I'll find something to run you in for. Get moving."

His face turns beet red and he guns the engine of his car. He pulls out of his parking place and slowly drives off as the woman counts her money.

"Fuckin' cops," she says as she stalks off. "Finally good for something."

At 4 P.M. on a cold Sunday, my young fire trainees and I are returning our truck to its garage. We have had a fine afternoon. We beat the fire company to a trash fire and had it out before the regular engines could arrive. The firemen might have been mad at us, but just at that moment they received a more serious call for a building fire. So they were happy to congratulate the boys on a job well done and speed off with a wave.

I am driving the truck along Adrian Street in Staten Island. The road is winding and bumpy. I cut the speed of the engine to about twenty miles per hour. We hit another bump or two, and suddenly I am aware of frantic yelling from the boys behind.

I slow down to a crawl. "What's going on?" I shout to them.

Then in the rearview mirror I see a figure sprawled across the roadway where we have just been.

As I slam on the brakes, my heart is in my throat. The boys leap off the truck and race back toward the body on the asphalt.

Then I realize that it is a boy from the truck. One of them loosened his grip or was changing hands when he hit a bump and he was jounced off.

I leap from the truck and run back. It is Michael.

He is not moving when I get near him. "Out of the way! Out of the way!" I yell in an uncharacteristic, frantic manner as I kneel down. I see immediately that he has grazed his skull. I can see the blood. I do not know how bad the injury is.

"Michael? Michael!" I cry out.

One of the older boys runs to the truck and jumps into the driver's seat. He puts on the lights and begins to back toward us. Another boy runs down the street fifty feet to hold up any cars that may be coming.

"Michael!" I beg again, trying to revive him. But he will only moan. I figure we are only ten minutes away from St. Vincent's Hospital in Staten Island, a place I know well.

I lift Michael and carry him in my arms to the truck. The boys help him aboard, just as we have practiced so many times before.

Al Ciponi drives the truck. "St. Vincent's!" I yell. The siren on our thirty-year-old warhorse cranks to life and we are on our way.

Michael is moaning and moving now, as if coming out of a deep narcosis. I cradle his upper body and my eye looks up and down for injuries that I have not yet noticed.

"Easy, Mike," I say to him. "Don't try to move."

He speaks groggily. He moves one leg but not the other.

I am thoroughly scared. I have been shot at twice in my life. I have disarmed at least seventy men with loaded guns. I have taken knives from more people than I care to remember, have clambered about on bridges as well as on skyscrapers, and been dragged by a speeding car. This moment, however, is the most terrifying of my life.

"Bill . . . ?" Mike asks me, looking up.

"It's okay, Mike. You're going to be okay." I promise him. And now that he is talking, I truly believe he will be. I mumble a silent prayer.

We arrive at the hospital emergency room. Two doctors attend to him, take X rays, and patch the visible damage. Michael is conscious now. But one leg, he says, will not move. It will not obey simple commands. The doctors are mystified. Somewhere, they theorize, there is neurological damage that has escaped their detection. The doctors and nurses remain busy around him for several hours.

Night falls. I see Michael in his hospital bed.

"What the heck were you doing back there?" I ask. "Didn't I teach you how to hold on?"

He nods. "I was switching hands," he said. "That's when we hit that bad bump."

"How's the leg?" I ask.

He shrugs. "It doesn't feel too bad. But there's this funny sensation."

"Tingling?"

He nods. "And real numb down there further." He points.

"Be brave, Michael," I say to him. "You got through some tough times before. You can do it again."

"Yeah, I know."

For the first time since the beginning of October, we are apart. I do not sleep well that night. As I dream I am again at the wheel of the fire truck. I hit the same bump, I hear a scream, my son is lying on the asphalt of the roadway and I bolt upright in bed. It is a long night. The house seems strangely empty.

The next morning I am back at the hospital. Michael is again a center of activity. I sit patiently, when permitted to be near him, and watch him undergoing these tests.

The doctors and nurses buzz around my seventeen-year-old, asking him what hurts and where, and how exactly he came to be riding on a fire truck. Each time he recounts the episode, it gets better.

Two nurses, one on each side of the bed, ask if he is comfortable and if there is anything they can do for him.

"No, ma'am," he replies in his most exaggerated Tennessee drawl. "But thank you very kindly for asking."

Son of a gun, I say to myself. The little conniver is enjoying this!

I stand up and walk toward the door.

"Hey, Bill?" he asks. "Where you going?"

"Just out for some air," I tell him. "I'll be right back."

I am out in the corridor and, I suppose, I should be outraged. But instead I'm relieved.

Then I see one of Michael's doctors.

"Hey, doc?" I ask. "Level with me. What's going on with my boy here?"

The doctor looks me in the eye, then shakes his head. "We're still working on it," he says. He wants to let it go with that, but I catch something in his eye. I ask him to tell me more. "Frankly," he continues, "it doesn't completely make sense. When he came in yesterday, he was shaken up, bruised, and scared. That could account for his problems yesterday and last night."

"How about today?" I ask.

He shrugs and shakes his head. "To be honest with you, we're somewhat baffled. The numbness seems to come and go from certain areas. I thought there was partial paralysis at first. But there isn't. And the X rays show no damage."

"If I didn't love the kid, I'd strangle him," I say with a grin.

The doctor cocks his head.

"He's getting a lot of attention, isn't he?" I ask.

"Well, yes. But—"

"Doc," I say, "I haven't been to medical school, but I think I can diagnose this for you. Got a minute?"

In a vacant room just off the corridor I tell the doctor Michael's story. "You've got to realize," I conclude, "that Mike went from getting no attention at all to being in the center of attention in New York City. All overnight."

He nods and manages to smile. "I'll let you handle it," he says. "But don't forget. The boy took a bad fall. In a way, it's understandable."

Moments later, I am back in Michael's room.

"How you feeling?" I ask.

"It's still numb," he says. "I dunno. It doesn't hurt bad or anything. Maybe..."

"Maybe what, Mike?"

"Maybe if I stay here for a couple more days, it'll go away."

"No, Michael," I tell him, "I'm afraid it's more serious than that."

A moment passes. "Is it?" he asks.

"It is," I affirm. "You see, this is just a little hick hospital in Staten Island. These doctors here, I mean, they're fine. Don't get me wrong. But the best ones are back at Bellevue."

"I have to go back to Bellevue?"

"As long as you can't get feeling in parts of your legs, we really have no choice. It's back to Bellevue for some thorough testing. It shouldn't take more than a couple of weeks."

"Wait a minute. That's going to be really expensive! You shouldn't—"

"We have your trust fund. That's what it's for, remember? Health and education."

Mike is flustered. "Bill, that's ridiculous!" he protests. "I don't need all those tests."

"Michael," I say patiently, rising to leave. "We're only trying to do what's best for you."

"What if the feeling comes back in my leg?"

"Oh, I doubt if that will happen at this point," I conclude. "But if it does, of course, you can come home." He stares at me, his suspicions building. "Say hello to the nurses for me. I like the red-headed one, myself. See you tomorrow."

When I return at noon the next day, Michael's bags are packed. He is up and walking around, waiting for me. His symptoms have miraculously disappeared.

"Feeling better?" I ask with a tone of surprise.

"I feel great,' he says. "All better."

I put my arm around his shoulders and cannot help laughing. "Then let's go home," I say.

If only it were always so easy.

* * *

Gary and I are walking through a rubble-strewn lot in the West Twenties. It is after seven in the evening on a winter night cold enough to keep the garbage in the lot all frozen together. Footing is difficult. The lighting is impossible. Gary and I are about thirty feet apart, joined by two officers from the Tenth Precinct. We are looking for a pistol used in a robbery. The suspect was apprehended two blocks away. He ran through this lot and came out of it without his weapon. It is in here somewhere.

A sergeant from the Ten house arrives in a sector car and looks at Gary and me. "Which one of you is Fox?" he asks, stepping out of his vehicle.

"I am," I say.

"You didn't answer the radio in your van," he tells me. The R.E.P. is half a block away.

"Better call your precinct. You got some sort of problem."

"What sort of problem?" I ask.

"Something personal. That's all I know."

I turn and walk quickly to the R.E.P., where I radio in. The news is short and sweet.

"Apparently everything's okay, Billy," Sgt. Givern tells me from the telephone in the one truck. "So don't get alarmed . . ."

"What the hell's going on," I hear myself beginning to shout. "I'll decide if I want to get alarmed."

"Your house caught fire. The local ladder company went over right away. You don't have much damage."

"What about—"

"Michael's fine. Your mother's okay, too. They had to give her some oxygen, though. She was pretty shook up and— Hey, Fox?"

The sergeant gives me emergency leave for the night and I don't even bother to go into the precinct to change.

*   *   *

I have a red flasher in my car and I throw it up onto the roof, Kojak-style. As I take off across the Brooklyn-Queens Expressway and over the Verrazano Narrows, there are a million thoughts shooting through my head. I don't like any of them. I have at least twenty minutes en route to calm down.

But I do not calm down very much.

I bring the car to a skidding halt on Targee Street, just by Van Duzer where I live. I jump out and turn the corner. My block looks exactly the way I left it. Even the front of my house looks the same.

I bolt through the door and every light in the house is ablaze. Straight ahead of me there are people in the kitchen. I see my brother and my sister, Eileen. I see Michael at the kitchen table. I see my cousins, Carol and Red Kenicky, who live next door.

I storm through the front hall and enter the kitchen, where Michael is holding court, telling people how he was the hero of the day.

"What the hell's going on here?" I ask. "Everyone all right?"

I look at my mother in particular, who gives me a nod. She sits in front of a cup of coffee, a cigarette in her hand. I watch her hand. It is unsteady. The others at the table look at me as if I am a madman.

"We told the guys at the precinct not to bother you," Eileen says.

"Where was the fire?" I demand.

"Downstairs," Ma says.

I walk to the door that leads to the basement and go down the steps.

The acrid odor of ashes and water is strong. The floor is still wet.

213

In one corner of the room is what remains of four pink rolls of fiberglass insulation. They had been piled on top of each other and the last time I saw them they were on the other side of the basement.

A charred area surrounds the one-hundred-watt overhead light. I look at the bare light bulb, reach up, and touch it. It is the same bulb that has been in that fixture for several weeks.

I turn the light off and return to the kitchen.

"What happened?" I ask.

Mike gives me the story very concisely. He was home alone. It was, in fact, the first time since he had been with us that he'd been home alone in the evening. I was on my first set of four-to-midnight shifts since the madness of the autumn. Ma had been out to dinner with friends.

"I was in the living room doing my homework," Mike elaborates. "And I smelled smoke from downstairs."

Mike tells me that he went to the cellar door, then ventured halfway down the steps. He got just far enough to see the fiberglass rolls piled high and leaning against the hundred-watt bulb. And the heat from the bulb, he ventures, ignited the insulation.

"Then what?" I ask.

"Then I ran next door to get Red," Mike says.

"That's right, Billy," Red confirms. Red called the fire company, who came sweeping around the corner within three minutes. But by that time, Red and Mike had charged back into the house with fire extinguishers from the Kenicky's home and stifled the flames.

I look at Michael enjoying his role of hero of the day and can barely control my temper.

"Mike," I say tersely, "we're going upstairs. I want to talk to you."

His expression sinks from one of heroism to one of fear. He doesn't move.

"Come on!" I order. "Let's go! Now!"

"Billy, what's the matter with you?" Ma asks. Eileen and the others are speechless.

"Stay right where you are," I say. "This won't take long."

Upstairs in my den, I tell Michael to sit down.

"Mike," I begin, "there's a lot of stuff I can let you get away with. Little mistruths, faking this and that, turning off the Atari when you're losing. But a fire isn't one of those little things."

He looks at me with big, pleading brown eyes. "I don't know what you mean," he says.

"I want the truth, Michael."

"I told you the truth," he begins. "I was in the living room when—"

I hold up my hand to stop him. "I'm not listening to you right now, Mike," I say to him. "I'm going to give you time to think about this. I'm coming back in a few minutes. Then I'd better hear a different story."

I take a long look at my foster son and I am not smiling. I leave the room and close the door behind me and walk back downstairs. The family is silent, watching me from the kitchen.

"I'll be back in twenty minutes," I tell them.

At the firehouse on Grand Street, I find Captain Tom Driscoll, one of my friends at that house.

"Tom," I ask him, catching him alone in the office, "you guys had a call at my house tonight. What was the story?"

He looks at me and rubs his chin. "Well, Bill," he hesitates, "you know, I suppose it was an accident. The light bulb was on for a while. The insulation was piled too close." He shrugs.

"Tom," I say, "don't bullshit me. I keep that light off. And the insulation was on the other side of the room when I left it."

"Look, no one was hurt. I'm marking it an accident."

But Tom Driscoll knows me too well. He also knows Michael and he knows Michael's problems.

"I've been a volunteer fireman and a professional cop too long to believe any tall tales, Tom," I press. "You know damned well that if the light bulb had started the fire the glass from the bulb would have melted or shattered. Right?"

He hesitates. "I don't want to say the boy started the fire, Bill," he tells me. "He was home alone and he called us. He had the fire out before we arrived. If he really wanted to damage your home, he had plenty of opportunity."

"Thank you, Tom."

"I'm classifying it as an accident," he repeats. But I am already on my way out of his office.

Back home I march straight upstairs. Michael is still in my den, exactly where I left him. I pull up a chair and sit down a few feet away from him.

"All right," I say. "I'm listening."

Now he begins to cry. "I...I don't know any more," he says.

I feel both anger and compassion as I look at him. I will make it easier for him, but I don't plan to let him off. "Mike, I want you to look me in the eye."

He obeys. His eyes are wet and red and his face streaked with tears. He does not know what to expect.

"Let me tell you one thing," I begin. "You're in our family now. You're not in Tennessee and you're not in North Carolina. I love you as I'd love my own son. And as far as the rest of the family is concerned, you are my son. But I want to know how that fire started."

He is breaking down again, crying even harder.

"You are going to tell me the truth, because I *know* how it started. Just like I know how the one in Tennessee started—with the lighter fluid on the draperies."

"I...I don't know. I can't..." he sobs.

"I will not put up with a liar, a thief, or a sneak in my household," I tell him. "I have to deal with it on the streets where I can't control it. But there's no reason for it in this house. Now, let's hear the truth."

He crosses the room, puts his arms around my shoulders, and sobs.

"I'm sorry," I can hear him saying. "I didn't mean it. I didn't mean to hurt anyone. I...I was here alone. I don't know why...I just wanted some attention, I guess...I'm sorry..."

He continues to cry, hard and loud. He comes completely clean, about this fire and the one in Tennessee, two confessions that he has never made to anyone before.

I place a hand on his shoulder. As angry, as infuriated as I am, I am torn with compassion. I know how terrified the boy must be at being left alone for even a few hours.

"I'll never do it again," he cries. "Trust me, Bill. Please. Never ever again."

I let him cry it out. I have to gather my own emotions, also. Then I say "You're going to do two other things tonight, Mike. You're going to stop smoking cigarettes in this house. You've forfeited your right to light a match here."

"All right," he cries. "All right."

"And you're going to take a first step toward becoming a man. You must own up to what you did today."

He wipes his eyes and looks at me. "I just did," he says. "I just told you."

I am shaking my head. "Not just me," I say. "You must go downstairs to those people. To the other members of your family. You must tell them what you did and that you're sorry."

"Oh, no," he says, the tears starting to flow again. "No. I can't."

"You have to, Mike. You're two months away from your eighteenth birthday. I'm sorry. I can give you a home but I can't give you your childhood back. You have to grow up tonight. You must act your age."

"I can't look them in the eye. How can I? After everything they done—"

"You've got to accept responsibility."

"You're going to ruin me," he pleads. "What are you going to do? Tell everyone in the Fire club what I done? Are you going to tell all your friends—Gary and Shep and the Giant?"

I consider it. "No," I say to him. "As far as anyone outside the house is concerned, the fire started with a cigarette or with the light bulb. You take your pick and I'll support your story. But as far as the family is concerned, you've got to come clean. These are people who love you and sacrifice for you and to whom you owe the truth."

I step to the door and open it. We can both see the stairway that leads down to the living room and the kitchen.

"It's time, Mike," I say. "You know what you got to do. I know it's not easy but you got to go down there."

I give him a minute or two to collect himself. Then he walks down the stairs in front of me. We go to the kitchen, where the family members, still completely mystified, are waiting. I let Michael enter the kitchen first and stand behind him as he speaks.

"The fire didn't start the way I told you before," he begins in an agonized, emotional voice. "The fire started because I set it, myself."

I watch the outrage increasing on the faces of those in the kitchen. From behind Michael I gesture to them to let Michael speak. I am convinced that this is the most difficult thing he has ever had to do. I want him to get through it.

"Michael, you could have killed someone!" Eileen says after he finishes.

"We've given you a home," my mother tells him with a shaking voice, only a shade away from breaking. "And you nearly destroyed it."

Michael hangs his head and is crying again. He turns to look at me. I am behind him but I am saying nothing. He is out there on his own, facing up to what he did.

He looks back to the family. "I know," he says, gathering his courage. "I know what I did. I told Bill I'll never do it again. Ever. I mean it." I know Michael. And I know when he *does* mean it.

There is a pack of Marlboros on the kitchen counter. They are Mike's and there is a book of matches with them. I take them, crush them in my hand, and drop them into the garbage.

My brother-in-law, Mike O'Connell, who has seen as much of the streets as I have, says nothing. He shakes his head and blows out a long, exhausted breath of air.

"Okay," I say, breaking several seconds of ominous silence. "Case closed. I think this matter is settled."

It is a night that will lie heavily on the memory of all of us. But if Michael can get through it, I tell him, so can we. A time of crisis is a time to pull together, no matter how hard that sometimes seems.

A few days later, Michael and I see his psychiatrist. "I think we've passed a milestone," he says to me after Mike's session. "You handled it well."

"Think so?" I ask. "I didn't know whether I came down on

219

him too hard or too soft. Plus, I'm still emotionally drained from it, myself."

"You must look at it from Mike's perspective," he answers. "He's done the worst things he can: the bedwetting and setting a household fire. Both either got him beaten or removed from a home. But you didn't throw him out and he didn't feel the need to run away. He knows you still love him. He's more secure than ever now."

I feel in need of a little help myself at the moment. "It's a tough way to test for security, isn't it?" I ask.

The doctor shrugs. "It's a tough case, Mr. Fox," he says. "But you knew that when you took Michael on."

"Any idea what may be next?"

"Next?" he ponders reflectively. "Next? I don't know. There might never be a 'next' this significant again. You made him take a big step forward. A *very* big step forward."

And the doctor is right. Suddenly many of the tensions have disappeared. Michael is calmer, more at peace with himself and with his new life. Even at school there are fewer problems. His grades improve, even in math.

I feel like a proud father. I am winning the important battle. The psychiatrist cuts back the visits to one a month.

It is a brutal Saturday in February. At the Explorers' Post the boys learn some elementary lessons in winter fire fighting when we aid two regular engine companies at a real fire.

"Fire and ice, Bill," a boy says to me as we are leaving. "Is that the hardest situation to come up against in regard to fire?"

Michael is nearby, listening for my response.

"That's *one* of the most difficult," I say.

Eighteen

FEBRUARY is the month of vehicle collisions on icy expressways and having to extricate the victims. It is older people slipping on sidewalks and being rushed to hospitals with broken hips. It is people trapped in elevators because ice has short-circuited the electricity running from the rooftop controls.

Gary Gorman is out with a sprained wrist and I am working with Bobby Benz, on one-day loan from Bronx Emergency Services. It is not yet 9 A.M. when Bobby and I receive our first call.

"EMERGENCY BOY-ONE," the division radio crackles. "CAN YOU GIVE US YOUR LOCATION?"

I reach for the radio. Benz is driving. I talk. "This is Emergency Boy-One, Central. We're at One Six Street and Three Avenue."

A split second later Central comes back on "EMERGENCY BOY-ONE, WE'VE GOT A TEN FIFTY-TWO AT TWELVE STREET AND

221

AVENUE C. SECTOR CARS FROM NINE PRECINCT ALREADY ON THE SCENE. CAN YOU ASSIST? TEN FOUR."

"We got it, Central. Ten four."

Benz and I barely look at each other. We know our jobs. A ten fifty-two is an individual on a ledge or a rooftop threatening to jump. My pulse begins to race and I know Bobby's does also. I hit the emergency lights on our van and he hits the gas. I give the siren a shot or two. We are moving downtown.

Moments ago I was thinking how tired I was. I have not slept well for the past two weeks. I feel as if I have been awake for two days straight, though I haven't. But now the adrenalin starts to flow.

We arrive two minutes later and hop out of the van. A sergeant from the Nine is on the scene. There is no jumper. Not anymore.

"You're in time to pick up some pieces," the sergeant tells us off-handedly. "He's around back of the building."

"Dead?" I ask.

The sergeant lights a cigarette and shakes his head. "No, but he ain't gonna be runnin' off nowhere, either."

The sergeant is a dark-haired, sharp-featured man named Eichel. He has little love for the man who lies in a painful heap at the rear of a slum tenement in the East Village. His lack of compassion is understandable.

"We been looking for this son of a bitch for two months," he says. "I had two men on it. Now I can put them on something important."

Sgt. Eichel leads us through an alley. We step over broken bottles and burned-out mattresses and bags of garbage that have obviously spent the winter lying against the building.

"We had two warrants out for this man for child abuse,"

222

the sergeant explains. "Two detectives followed him to his apartment. Common-law wife and child live there. Our detectives went to the front door so the guy crawled out the fourth-story window with some sheets."

We are led to a man who lies on a stretch of concrete at an impossible angle. His legs are folded under him as if he were a contortionist. He is moaning and two officers are administering first aid to him. An ambulance has been called. The officers are from the Ninth Precinct. One is white and one is black. The man, somewhere in between, mutters incoherently in Spanish. He wants a cigarette. He is racked with pain, the police have captured him, his legs are broken, and he will probably go to jail after the hospital. But all he can think of now is a cigarette.

The sergeant finishes. "He tried to come down on the sheets from the fourth-story window." We look up toward it and see a dozen or so neighbors leaning on their window sills calmly watching the morning entertainment. They chatter to each other. "But he only had two sheets and they didn't hold him anyways. So he fell from about forty feet."

There is nothing we can do and we are about to be dismissed when a patrolman from the Nine runs over to us. "Hey, sarge," he says urgently, "we got a problem."

Sgt. Eichel looks at him and says nothing.

"The woman has gone wacko. She's barricaded in the apartment and she's threatening to throw the kid out the window."

"Jesus Christ," the sergeant mutters. He spits away his cigarette. "I thought we could get out of here." He looks at us. "Come on," he says.

Now the situation becomes our ball game. Neighbors tell a Spanish-speaking officer that the woman has been in and out of Bellevue Psychiatric. They point to their heads and revolve their fingers telling us that the woman is crazy. But, yes indeed, she has her three-year-old child in there, the child whom the father has abused. The plunge her husband took has set her off. She plans to throw her child out the window.

"She's done it before!" one of the neighbors tells us joyfully. Everyone laughs because they know the police will now provide a show.

Benz and I run to our truck. We radio for an emergency back-up team, and an airbag to be set up under the window. We race up the stairs just as another team arrives. Other officers are at the woman's door trying to distract her or talk some sense into her. She is shrieking from the inside. I cannot understand her.

Benz and I gain access to the apartment above the woman. We go to the rear of the building, directly above the window from which the woman has threatened to throw her child. In our hands is a heavy section of netting.

I look out. Underneath the window the ambulance attendants are removing the man who fell. A few feet away from him other Emergency cops are inflating a thirty-foot airbag. For a second I think how unreal it looks. One crew finishing up, the other just arriving. But there isn't any more time to think. Only to act.

Benz and I drop one end of the net. We hold our end and pull it tightly through the window. We feel a tug on the other section. Cops in the apartment two flights below have grabbed the net and are pulling it in. Benz and I tie our lines tourniquet-tight. We now have cut off the disturbed woman's window. Over it there is a nylon mesh through which she can throw nothing.

A precinct cop is in our path as we leave the apartment to go downstairs. "Do you guys have the battering ram?" he asks.

"We got to get the door open. She could be carving up the kid by the time we get in."

"There's a battering ram in both trucks," I tell him. "Aren't the other guys bringing it up?"

"I'll see," he says, and hurries off while Benz and I go to the locked door, where two precinct cops appear to be waiting. The woman is still screaming from within.

"The other emergency guys went for the ram," one tells us. Something on his face says that he *wants* to watch us break down a door.

A fat little man in an undershirt stands at the end of the corridor.

"Who's that guy?" I ask.

"The superintendent," someone says.

I turn toward him and he gives me an amiable smile. This is his building and he, too, seems to want to see a door smashed in.

"Hey, buddy," I say to him. "Who's got the keys to these apartments?"

"Me," he answers.

"You?"

He gives us a wistful smile as he reaches into his pocket and produces a set of master keys for the building. He could have volunteered them half an hour ago. But he prefers a specific invitation.

The Emergency men arrive with the battering ram. "Don't bother," Benz tells them.

I turn the key and the door opens. We draw our pistols just in case, but the crisis has passed. The woman has set her child down on a floor that is not much more orderly than the alley outside. The little boy is playing with an empty milk carton. His mother is shrieking at the net that has covered her windows.

225

From here the precinct men take over. There is no weapon and no fight. Just an hysterical woman and a child with little hope for a tomorrow any more promising than today.

Benz and I are packing our nets back into the truck when we get a second call. Another jumper. Only this time he has already done it—from the thirty-second floor. And this time it isn't a roach farm in the East Village, but the United Nations.

We check our gear as quickly as possible and shoot to the F.D.R. Drive. Our lights are on again and we move through traffic that, despite the lights and the siren, does not always want to move for us. I do not have time to reflect on the man with two broken legs in a heap behind the tenement in the East Village, the twisted psyche of his common-law wife, battered by a lifetime of slums and unemployment, or the peculiar logic that tells the woman that things will improve if only she can heave her three-year-old out the window. I can only entertain the depressing notion that this child will probably be the father's biological replacement in more ways than one.

As we turn from the Drive onto the grounds of the United Nations, there is no mystery as to where the body landed. A crowd of security people surround it as well as two blue-and-white NYPD cars.

I think back, trying to assure myself that I saw a body bag in the rear of the truck when we began our shift. I *know* I saw one. "Thirty-two fucking floors," I mumble to Benz. "We may need the shovels for this one."

We park our truck as close to the spot as possible. We are on the sidewalk right by the huge plate glass skyscraper section of the U.N. The security people are assessing the dead man or exchanging pleasantries with each other.

There is a sheet covering the body. I walk to it. Benz removes the orange body bag from the rear of the R.E.P. The security people look at me without speaking.

226

I see familiar faces and stances, though I know none of these men by name, and can tell the Secret Service from the F.B.I. and the F.B.I. from the private United Nations Security.

"What happened?" I ask.

One of the Secret Service agents says, "He was a Dutch economic attaché. Who knows what was bothering him. He jumped from an office at UNESCO." He shrugs as if to suggest that the details hardly matter. Come to think of it, they probably don't. Drugs? Alcohol? Money? Politics? Adultery? Homosexuality? Whatever the man's problems, they are over now.

I pull away the sheet, uncovering the face first, and look at the lifeless, inanimate features of a man about my own age. In his lifetime, which concluded thirty-six minutes ago, he had been handsome, with blue eyes and sandy blond hair. His body, though twisted, is still intact. But the skull is broken open.

"An *economic* attaché?" repeats one of the F.B.I men. "Hey, he must have known something." Everyone's emotional defenses are in high gear. "Sell those stocks," someone else remarks. "Wall Street's crashing again."

We lift the body into the bag and the precinct cops help us as the men from other agencies join in the jokes. They are under no obligation to participate, and they don't. This is, after all, no longer a human being on the sidewalk. It is a cadaver, a job to be done, and it's not their job. So they play no part in it.

The truck from the morgue turns up as if on cue and I make a mental note to replace the body bag when our shift is over. A few minutes later we are on our way.

There are two police radios in our R.E.P. One is citywide. The other broadcasts to Special Operations Divisions only. Us, in other words. But we listen to both radios as we drive. We can tell when a job is about to shift from citywide to Emergency.

There is an incessant crackling on the citywide radio. Voices of dispatchers who I don't know and will never meet distribute bits of information to the various police agencies in the city nonstop. It is like a flood of bad news. A rape in Morningside Heights. An armed robbery in progress at a Citibank branch in Chelsea. An auto has jumped onto a sidewalk in Soho and skidded through a store window. A young man has collapsed on West Seventy-second Street; no one knows whether it's drugs, a heart attack, or a diabetic seizure. In Prospect Park a woman is hysterical because she seems to have lost her child somewhere in the park. No one can be quite sure because she is Indonesian, according to her expired passport, and speaks no English. Someone is speeding to the Indonesian Mission at the United Nations, not far from where we just were, to pick up a young man who has kindly offered to interpret. A patrol car will take him to Brooklyn where the local precinct, the seventy-seventh, will then try to determine what the problem is and solve it. Oh yes, a known prostitute has been found dead in the trunk of a car in the West Thirties. Natural causes are not suspected.

Now our own radio crackles to life "EMERGENCY BOY-ONE ARE YOU AVAILABLE?"

I reach for the radio. "This is Boy-One. What have you got?"

"EMERGENCY BOY-ONE, WE GOT A TEN SIXTY-EIGHT AT THE SUBWAY STATION AT EIGHT AVENUE AND FOUR-TWO STREET. THE TRAINS ARE STOPPED."

Benz and I look at each other and moan. But Bobby's foot is already on the accelerator.

"That's a heavy one, Central," I answer. "We'll need a solid back-up."

"AFFIRMATIVE, BOY-ONE," Central responds. "WE'RE ROLLING THE BIG TRUCK."

As we head toward the subway, the One Truck is roaring out of the garage at Twenty-first Street at the same time. The big truck carries every piece of heavy emergency equipment we own. For this job, we may need it all. Eleven minutes after we receive the ten sixty-eight, our R.E.P. arrives at Forty-second and Eighth Avenue.

Already there is chaos. Officers from the Midtown South and Midtown North precincts have set up a perimeter around the subway station, but crowds of the curious and the irritated are gathering. The subway has been blocked in both directions. There is a body under one of the trains.

We go down the stairs, pushing our way through the crowds. People either make way for us or shout at us, and not all the shouting is friendly. In a situation like this, we look for other blue uniforms. And, fortunately, just seconds later, other emergency men from other trucks arrive.

"The big truck is only a block away," Al Sheppard shouts to me.

"What happened?" Benz asks.

Transit officer Isaac Reynolds tells us. "A thirty-year-old male Hispanic was riding between the cars of the train. Must have leaned over when the train came into the station. He was picked off by the platform and got squashed." Reynolds is more concerned with the growing crowd than the dead man.

"How do you know he was Hispanic?" I ask for no good reason.

Reynolds shrugs. "See for yourself."

The upper half of the man's body is still wedged between a subway car and the platform. The lower half is scattered at various points underneath. It is our job to collect the pieces.

"Time for the rubber gloves," Benz says to me.

229

More cops flood into the station. The crowd is held back as best possible. People are jockeying for positions in order to see everything. Others have had their daily schedules upset by the man's death.

"What happened?" is the most frequent question I hear, though anyone who can see has no need to ask.

"When will the trains start running again?" is number two.

Richie Seaberg, Al Sheppard, and Mike Stapleton, all from our unit on Twenty-first Street, jockey the enormous inflatable airbag into an area beneath the train. Benz and I crawl down under the car and guide the bag into a position where the sharp wheels of the train will not slash it. The odor is indescribable. The smell of garbage and a sewer that leaks into these tracks persuades Benz and me to work quickly and efficiently. We use heavy emergency lamps to see.

The airbag is in place and we retreat to a safe distance. "Ready!" I shout. The work has been tedious and demanding. We mop the sweat from our faces and arms as an emergency cop on the platform lets go with a torrent of compressed air. As if by magic the airbag inflates, lifts the entire subway car, and gives us room to work.

The Emergency men on the platform grab the dead man's upper torso as the subway car leans backward and place it in a body bag. This is what the crowd was waiting for, yet now that they see it, many groan, scream, or turn away.

Bobby Benz and I go down under the car with a second body bag. What we must do is gruesome but routine. We find a severed leg. We place it in the bag. We see something odd perched on a rail and put my light on it. Wordlessly, I pick it up and put it in the bag with the leg. It was the man's ear. There is gore running for sixty feet beneath the train and slowly Benz and I and others gather up the indescribable remains, including part of a foot with part of a sneaker still tied onto it.

"Jeeze," somebody says. "And he had a brand new pair of Adidases, too."

There is ghoulish laughter under the train.

But what should be the response? How else can you approach it when a human being has been squashed to death? Taken on a strictly human level, you'll be ready for the nuthouse within minutes. We must account for the entire body before we leave. We actually inventory it. When a T.A. man finds the fingers, our inventory is complete. We can leave.

By chance, up on the street, I see the same crew from the Medical Examiner's office that were at the United Nations a few hours earlier. They are suprisingly cheerful men, considering their line of work. They give me a smile.

"Busy day, huh?" one of them says.

"You ain't kidding," I respond. And it's only three o'clock. We're still on duty.

At the end of our shift, a thirty by twenty-five foot advertising billboard collapses at Eighth Avenue and Fortieth Street. We do not have to travel far. There are no serious injuries, but several pedestrians have been struck by the debris. One or two will be hospitalized, but they are able to enter the ambulance under their own power. Happening on the heels of everything else this day, the billboard is almost comic relief.

By four-thirty I am back in the stationhouse, exhausted. A man can look at only so much during the day. And February, it seems, has just been one long terrible month of such days.

I remain at the Gray Table for an extra hour. Let the home-

231

ward traffic be damned. This afternoon I need to hang out and kick things around.

I am quiet. I listen to the other man. Jimmy Kontos, also on loan from the Bronx unit, describes in detail a similar subway accident he recalls from two years earlier, this one at the Grand Concourse.

"You know what?" he concludes. "I remember every detail and I can see the whole thing perfectly, but the other guys in my unit tell me I wasn't there. I just heard so many accounts of it that I began to see it myself. Now I can't forget it. I dream about it. And if put on a witness stand, I'd swear I was there, too."

Jimmy, also, is tired. Maybe Emergency in a nonstop city like this *is* too much for any human being.

When I get home at seven Michael is waiting for me.

"I guess you forgot," he says.

"Forgot what?" I ask.

"You and me were going to go to the movies tonight. Six o'clock show. Remember?"

"Oh gee, Mike," I begin, collapsing into the chair in the living room. "I'm knocked out. What about tomorrow?"

The sinking expression on his face betrays his disappointment. "You promised," he reminds me.

"Yeah, I know, but—"

"Never mind. It's okay," he says.

He is quiet through dinner and goes to his room early that night. No Atari. No television. I try to engage him in conversation, but fail. It is too late, of course, to make good on my earlier promise.

The next evening, I am home by five-thirty and I open the movie directory. "What do you want to see?" I ask.

"I can't do it tonight, Bill," he says. "Look at this." He

shows me a mountain of homework, "I'm too busy."

I understand. The rebuff is a valid one. A promise is a promise and I will never again break one to Michael. Trust is too fragile a commodity.

Nineteen

IN the middle of March, a reporter for the *New York Times* visits our home to write a feature article about Michael and me. We have a good time with the interview. Things have been going very smoothly recently. The problems that Michael had in the first few months have eased considerably.

The article appears on Monday, March 22. It is a good, accurate account of our life together. The writer mentions that Michael's trust fund now totals three thousand dollars, comprised of many generous contributions from cops, friends, and lots of total strangers. She also mentions a possible television movie based on the rooftop incident, as well as a book.

For a few days, Michael is a celebrity again at school. Then the weekend arrives. Mike's birthday is the following Monday. But we are celebrating this Saturday.

We go out to dinner in Staten Island, to a French restaurant in Ellingville. Michael shows off his working knowledge of

French and menus—a reminder of past wanderings and employment. Then we go over to New Jersey to see the film *Porky's,* ninety-six minutes of crass, coarse, juvenile entertainment. We both love it.

When we return to Staten Island and park, I know immediately that something is up. There are too many cars on the block. And there are too many lights on in the house. As I open the front door, three reporters leap to their feet, one from the Associated Press, one from the New York *Post* and one from the New York *Daily News.* A reporter from the Staten Island *Advance* arrives just as I do.

My mother is standing in the living room. "It's Michael's mother," she says. "She's been calling here all evening."

I almost explode. "She's been doing *what?*" I ask.

One of the reporters switches on a tape recorder as he brings me up to date. "It was in the Ft. Worth *Star,* Mr. Fox," he says. "Mike's mother says she loves him and wants to see him again."

"She says she knows it's his birthday and she wishes him well," another says.

I can feel Michael's discomfort immediately. I place a protective hand on his shoulder.

"It's going to be in the papers tomorrow," one of them continues. "What about it? Do you want Michael to see her?"

"What do you think, Mike?" someone asks. "Would you like to see your mother again?"

Before Michael can answer, I intervene. "First of all," I tell them, "Mike will make his own decision about seeing his mother. And second, tonight we're celebrating Mike's eighteenth birthday. This is a family occasion. None of you were invited, so I'll thank all of you to leave."

But it is too late to salvage Mike's birthday. He retreats to his room. The birthday cake goes uneaten.

"I don't want to see that woman," he tells me tearfully. "Not at all. Not ever."

But I know things will not be so easy. I have been at Michael's bedside too often and I have discussed his mother with him too many times. I know the torment. I know the curiosity that lurks beneath his rage. I know the uncertainties of this boy who thinks his mother never loved him but hopes that in some way she does. It is the final demon that Michael must confront. And it is titanic.

He is red-faced and he is crying. "Why couldn't she leave me alone?" he asks. "Why does she have to start now?"

Monday is Michael's birthday and it too is ruined.

The newspapers carry pictures of Michael's mother with her two other sons. They smile out from a happy domestic pose deep in the heart of Texas. In the text, Michael's mother wishes him love, although she says she thinks he does not love her. She says that until seeing Mike's picture in the news last week—syndicated by the New York Times News Service—she thought he was dead.

"What utter bullshit!" I mutter to myself when I read the article. I think back to the legal papers served on her in October and the conversation we had when I first took custody of Michael. "Now she comes forward," I curse to Gary as we do our tour of duty that day. "Now that he's legal age. Now that she's got no responsibility for him any more. Now that she thinks he's worth something."

School is no relief for Michael. His friends are divided. One half reminds him that the woman in Texas *is* his mother. He should visit her, they say, to see what his roots are. The other half believe she has no business bothering him again. She gave him up long ago, they feel, and has made no effort to find him for sixteen years.

Michael is torn by both arguments. When I get home, I find him alone in his room. He is sifting through the day's mail. Then he shows me. There are two letters from his maternal grandmother, a birthday card and a handwritten note. Enclosed are photographs of Michael's full brother, who is sixteen, and his half brother, who is eleven.

Wordlessly, Michael hands me the photographs. Each boy has written a personal note to Mike on the reverse side. Michael's full brother looks just like him. Michael is transfixed by the pictures.

"I never knew I'd really see them," Michael says slowly and thoughtfully. "I mean, Bill, they're brothers. I got real flesh-and-blood brothers."

I can imagine what Michael is going through. And I know he is being pulled away from me.

"What else?" I ask.

He shows me the rest. There is a picture of his female cousin, who died of leukemia two years earlier, according to the note. She is a smiling, slightly overweight blonde woman, standing with her husband in front of a car on a strip of tract housing. Clipped to the birthday card is a check.

"Enclosed is five dollars to prove that I love you," writes his grandmother.

"I don't know what to do, Bill," he says in real pain. "These folks are my kin. My real kin." He looks up at me as if I might have an answer.

I sit on the edge of the bed. "Whatever you do, Mike," I tell him, "you don't have to be rushed into any decision. They've waited a great many years to get in touch with you. You don't have to rush off to do anything for them."

"I guess," he answers.

We go out that night and I treat Michael to his first legal beer. It does nothing, however, to ease the tension.

On Tuesday, coming home from the eight-to-four shift, I find Michael reading a letter in the living room. This time the letter is not from a relative. Instead, it's from Mike's girlfriend at Curtis High School and is addressed to his mother. Michael hands it to me.

Handwritten on school notebook paper, it reads

To Mike Buchanan's Mother,

Do you feel that it's right to enter Mike's life again? It might have been right before or even after he is older. But now he's just starting a new life. He doesn't want to look back anymore. Please don't make him! He's grown so much since he's been here. I hate to see him so worried. Why can't you just leave him alone?

Mary Ann

I give the letter back to Michael and sit down beside him on the sofa. He is far away in thought.

"Mike, where'd you get this?" I ask.

"Mary Ann wanted me to address it to my mother," he says. "She gave it to me to mail."

"Aren't you going to send it?"

He thinks about it. "No," he says. "Think I should?"

"Probably not," I answer. "No use getting anyone else involved. I could write a letter, too, Mike. There are things I could say. These same things and more."

"Yeah? Like what?"

"After all these years, Mike, after she knew where you were way back in October, it's awfully funny that she appears the very day that you're no longer her legal responsibility."

"Yeah. I know."

"The day you're eighteen and one week after that newspaper article. The article also mentioned that you had a little money now."

"Yeah. I know that, too."

Mike takes the letter back from me, looks at it, then peevishly tears it up, drops it into the wastebasket, and walks to his bedroom.

"What do you want to do?" I ask him.

He plops himself down on the sofa and folds his arms. Then he reaches for the telephone and picks it up.

"I'm going to call Associated Press," he says. "I'm gonna tell them that I'm happy here. I don't want to see her."

Mike dials the phone right in front of me and is put through to the A.P. reporter. But there is a certain tension on his face, even after delivering his message. The evening is quiet. Later, I visit him after he has finished his homework to see what he is doing.

He is sitting on the bed, looking at the letters from his grandmother, and studying the photographs of his brother and half brother.

I stand in the doorway to his room and look in. "Still wondering about it, huh?"

"Would you stop me if I wanted to go down?"

"No, Michael. I wouldn't stand in your way. If you're curious, you have to make the decision whether to go or not."

He looks down again, intrigued by the two photographs. "It *is* family, you know. I mean, real family. It's the first time I ever seen real relatives in almost ten years."

"You're seeing the doctor tomorrow night, right?" I ask.

"Yeah."

"He's been helping you. Let's see what *he* thinks."

*   *   *

"It's a tough one," the doctor says to me in private the next night after Michael's session. "And you're very right about one thing: You can't stop him."

"The way I see it," I say to him, "is that if I stand in Michael's way, it will only create bigger problems later. He'll resent me for it." The doctor nods. "Maybe he should go and get it out of his system."

"There are two possibilities when he gets there," the doctor says. "He'll either be horrified at what he finds and he'll want to take the next plane back."

"Or?"

"Or he'll want to stay. You have to remember, Mike's a Southern boy at heart. There are a lot of pressures on him due to his celebrity status up here. He may find the whole pace of life more suitable down there. It's the chance you take if he goes."

I shake my head. "It's too damned bad," I say to the psychiatrist. "Mike was doing well here. He was straightening his life out. It's too bad she had to appear now. Maybe in a few months it would have been better."

"You're a police officer," he reminds me, steepling his hands in front of his face and peering at me through thick glasses. "You should know: It's a pretty imperfect world out there."

"Yeah," I tell him, "I know. There's just one thing that nags at me."

"What's that?"

"It's just my own opinion," I say. "But if that woman really cared about the welfare of Michael Buchanan, she would have left him alone."

"This coming week is Easter recess, isn't it?" the doctor

240

says. "You could send him down then. For the weekend, maybe. Tell him he's expected back to go to church with you on Easter. Make sure he has a couple of things scheduled that he enjoys doing. It will give him an added incentive to return."

"You think that will guarantee that he comes back?"

The doctor rolls his eyes and gives me a dubious expression. *"Nothing* guarantees that," he says. "But don't forget, you're in the same position of any man who's been a father."

"How so?" I ask.

"Sooner or later the kids leave home. And as tough as a man may be, he's never ready for it."

On Monday night the fifth of April we are driving toward LaGuardia Airport. Michael and I have thrashed out the situation for several days. He wants to meet his mother, brother, and half brother. That's all there is to it.

I have asked Shep to come along with us. Of all my friends on the force it is perhaps Sheppard who has been closest to Michael. But he is with us now not because of Michael.

"Let me get this straight," Shep said to me two hours earlier when I asked him to come. "A big rough-and-tumble E-man who's been through everything you have and now, with this kid, you're asking for moral support?"

"That's right. Can you be there?"

"Sure thing."

We arrive at the airport early in the evening. Michael is surprised that we are at LaGuardia. I told him that he'd be leaving from Newark. The last thing I want—the last thing he needs—is reporters. If he is to meet his mother for the first time in sixteen years, he should do it without a carnival atmosphere.

The three of us have dinner at the airport. I am nervous

without knowing why. My palms are moist. I tell myself that he is just leaving for a few days. I bought him a return ticket, after all. Why am I so anxious?

Michael is higher than a kite. I can tell by his incessant chatter. But the talk is healthy. He is talking of the Easter service when he returns, his girlfriend at Curtis, the choral group, going up to the Catskills with me in the summer. I *know* he will be back. Don't I?

Mike's flight number is called.

Shep waits in the departure lounge. Michael carries one of his bags and I carry the other. He wears the clothing we picked out together and as I steal a look at him from the corner of my eye, I cannot help thinking back to the frightened, under-nourished, unloved kid whom Gary and I grabbed off the roof last September.

We arrive at the gate.

"Okay, kid," I tell him. "Nervous?"

He hunches his shoulders. "A little."

"So am I," I say. We share a laugh, as we have so often.

"There are things you have to remember," I say to him. "Shall I run through them?"

"Shoot."

"When you get there, you're free to do whatever you want. I don't know your mother, so I have to abide by your judgment. If you want to stay there, you're free to stay. No hard feelings. She's your natural mother and I know that counts for something."

"I've always wondered about her," he says. "You know?"

"You just give me the word and I'll send your things down," I tell him. "Except for the tropical fish. They don't travel so well."

He grins.

"If things go the wrong way or if things don't seem right, you give me a call and climb on a plane. I'll be here waiting for you."

"Okay."

"There's just one thing you can't do, Michael." He waits and I continue. "The house here in Staten Island is a home. It's not a hotel. You're eighteen now and you've got to start making the hard decisions. If you want to stay in Texas, you can stay. If you want to come back, you can come back. But you can't bounce back and forth. I'm not letting you turn into a drifter like your father. I don't make too many rules, Michael, but that's one you'll have to respect."

"I know, Bill. I understand."

I offer him my hand but the handshake becomes an embrace. Mike's flight is called a second time. He picks up his two suitcases and gives me the big-ear-to-ear smile.

"See you," he says.

"See you," I answer.

Then I watch until he passes through security and disappears down the ramp.

Shep is suddenly beside me. "I think he'll be back," Shep says.

"With Michael," I answer, "I've learned to count on only one thing. The unexpected."

"I've learned something, too," Shep says.

"What's that?"

"You may look like a big tough cop, Billy. But you're really just a pussy cat. Come on," he says, "let's get out of here."

Two nights later, Michael and I have a long talk by phone. He likes his mother. He likes his two brothers. He likes Texas. "I want to give it a try down here, Bill," he tells me hesitantly.

243

"I know how much you done for me. But this...I don't know. It's my real family. They're my honest-to-God relations."

"You want me to ship your stuff down?"

"Could you?"

"Just be sure you're making the right decision, Mike," I tell him. "You know what's offered to you in New York. Be sure that Texas has something better."

"I want to give it a try," he tells me again.

"Mike," I say, "I'm always pulling for you and I'm always in your corner. So I hope you make it work."

It is only a matter of time before the press discovers that Michael has returned to his mother, and then the madness starts all over again—ringing telephone, reporters' questions, invitations to appear on television.

I'd be lying if I said it didn't hurt. But the painful parts of life are part of living. I am told by people that they feel sorry for me, that I provided a home that was too good for the boy, something he didn't deserve.

I laugh. Is there such a thing as being too generous? If there is, I will someday do it again.

A reporter from a weekly New York magazine comes to the house. She wants to do a story on Michael, on how he was involved in drugs at Curtis and how he ran off without telling me. Total lies.

Then somebody from the *Today Show* calls. They are flying Michael and his mother up to New York to appear. Would I care to be on television with them?

"You know," I tell them, "I'm not a performer. I'm a cop."

"We thought it would be nice," purrs a female voice.

"Just remind me to take off the make-up before I go into the precinct," I tell her. "I'll be there."

I work a late shift the night before and get home at 1 A.M. I am due at 30 Rockefeller Plaza, the television studio, at seven.

I am accompanied this morning by a writer friend who rarely gets out of bed before ten and who has difficulty meeting me by eleven. Today I find him punctually in the lobby of the RCA building at 6:59 A.M. I'm amazed.

At nine minutes after seven, the producer's assistant telephones Michael and his mother at the hotel where they are being put up by the network. They are still asleep.

"Well," says the assistant, glancing calmly at her watch, "you're on in fourteen minutes. Can you hurry over?"

They do. Three minutes before we go on, Michael comes out of the elevator, his mother in tow. She is a short, dark woman with Michael's face and coloring.

Michael draws her over. "Mom" he says, "this is Bill Fox."

I offer my hand and we shake. "Oh, hello," she says flatly. Then she looks away.

On the air, Bryant Gumbel interviews the three of us for less than five minutes. In response to his direct question, and looking at him not me, Michael's mother says she is "very grateful" to have her lost son back.

Michael and his mother then return to Texas.

Epilogue

THE lunacy of the summer comes quickly this year. By mid-June the annual heat-inspired insanity is upon the city. Gary and I are called to a steaming apartment in the East Village where a woman has barricaded herself. She has a butcher knife and has announced that she will carve up her children. Gary and I, wearing our regular bullet-proof vests with flak jackets over our shirts, pick the lock of the apartment. It must be a hundred degrees. Sweat rolls off us and there is no light. I enter first. When the woman steps out of a closet behind me, a knife held aloft, I do not see her. Gary grabs her hand before she drives the blade into my neck.

Mike and I speak over the telephone once or twice a week. I am no longer happy with the sound of his voice. I sense something has changed since he first traveled down to Texas, but he assures me everything is fine. He tells me he has obtained a driver's license. I shudder. And he also tells me that he's getting an equivalency diploma from high school because he is over eighteen and they won't let him back into the school system. I grimace. Curtis is a good school. He was doing well there. And his teachers were helping him.

I ask Michael's mother and stepfather about his psychiatric care.

"He seems just fine to us," one of them says. I remind them that there is money for such care. All they have to do is give me the name of the doctor and I will make the payments out of Michael's trust account.

"We don't believe much in that stuff," they tell me.

The nineteenth of June is my birthday. I am five years older this year than I was last year at this time, although the calendar will only count one. In the mail arrives a greeting card on the front of which is a saddled horse hitched to a gasoline pump. Above the horse is the inscription:

A cowboy says that in this world you need just two things,
A good horse and a good friend.

Inside the message concludes:

Happy birthday, friend!

Below, in Mike's handwriting, is the letter *L,* as if he'd started a word but didn't finish. The single letter is followed by his name.

The next day, first thing on a Sunday morning, the telephone rings. Mike is calling to wish me well. After all, it's June twentieth. Father's Day.

In July, the Big Apple bakes. There is too much going on. Too much heat, too much madness, too much violence. Every horrible thing I see I have seen before and will probably see again. My instincts and wishes become very simple. I merely want to see my way through the summer. For some reason, I feel autumn will bring something better. I don't know why.

But in August our luck fails. Gary and I are chasing a suspect on the Lower West Side. Gary follows the man up a fire escape. The ladder is old and corroded. A rung gives way. Gary plunges two and a half flights. Miraculously he survives, but his hip is gone. Before the month is out, a department surgeon examines Gary and pronounces the injury too disabling for him to remain on the force. I forget what the suspect we were chasing had done. But I do know I have lost the best partner with whom I've ever served.

Nor is August a good month for Michael. On a muggy night midway through the month, he calls me.

"Hi," he says. "How are things going?"

"I'm okay," I answer.

"How's the leg?" he asks, referring to an accident I'd had in the spring.

"I'm getting around with all the grace and speed of Chester on *Gunsmoke.*"

"You never were real fast," he teases.

"I managed to grab you, didn't I?"

We laugh and he continues. "I wanted you to know," he drawls, "I'm hitting the road."

Suddenly serious I ask, "What's the matter, Mike?" I definitely do not like the tone of his voice.

"Don't get alarmed," he chides. "I saved up some money. I'm going backpacking out West with some friends."

"You going to stay out of trouble?"

"I'm gonna try," he promises. "I may go to the Fair in Knoxville. I'd like to see Tennessee again."

He draws a breath. "The way I see it," he says, "I know who I am better now. I know who my dad was. I know who my mom is. I know my brothers and my mom's mother. I got a better sense of everything."

"You coming to the Northeast?" I ask.

"You never know."

"You got my telephone number if you have a problem, Mike. And you're always welcome here."

"I know, Bill. Thanks."

I think back to my own father. I'm like any other man whose son is out there on his own. I am proud but I also worry. I know the things that can happen, but I know he can take care of himself. Though I wish some things had turned out differently, I did the best I could. I can lend a boy a hand with his future, but I cannot control his fate.

"Bill," he concludes, "I want you to know something."

"Yeah?"

"I, um...I, uh..."

Why, I wonder, is it always so difficult to say what one most wants to express. He retreats. "I know you done a lot for me," he says. "I won't forget it."

"I love you, too, Mike," I tell him.

"Thanks," he says.

Two days later, with a knapsack across his back, Michael sets out with some friends heading West.

The first card I receive bears a Tucson postmark. I am apprehensive. I am not a mind reader but I believe I know Mike better than anyone else. It is only a matter of time.

About two weeks later, I arrive home at 2 A.M. A cop had been injured and I'd gone with him to Bellevue. Ma is waiting up for me, even though I had called and told her not to. But when I see her face, I know something is amiss.

"What's going on?" I ask.

"You had a phone call," she says. "Several."

"The precinct?"

"Michael," she says. "He's in North Carolina. He's broke. He wants to know if you'll really let him come back."

I take a long breath and plop into the reclining chair in our living room. My eyes are stinging they are so tired. Every muscle in my body aches. Ma stands and watches me until she sees a smile cross my face.

"That's what I thought," she says. "Good night, Billy."

I am in the waiting room at LaGuardia Airport. Thoughts and images race through my mind so rapidly that I can neither count nor connect them. They are upon me and then they are gone, like the dreams I used to have.

It is a few days before Labor Day and, mercifully, the summer is almost over. I have again seen too much. I have probably tried to do too much. I have lost my partner and I have begun to wonder how many more summers it will be before some crazy accident catches up with me. Then I dismiss the notion. I have seen little over the hot months that reaffirms ultimate human goodness. Yet I still believe in it. I suppose that's what faith is all about.

Too edgy to sit down in the waiting room, I remain on my feet, glancing every few minutes at the ARRIVALS board. Mike's flight has landed. I turn my attention toward the gate, but there are no passengers yet.

A year has passed since the incident at the Fulton Hotel. It hardly seems possible. How could so much, good and bad, be packed into twelve months? I remember what friends of mine with children have always said. A year passes so quickly in the life of a son or daughter. You blink and it's gone. So you try not to blink.

All at once I see my own father as I still remember him. Strong and tall, filled with love and dedication for his family. When I was growing up, I had the type of relationship with my father that I've witnessed in so many other Irish-American homes. There was a immensely strong bond between us, something that remained unspoken yet that I knew I could always rely on.

That's what I was lucky enough to have had. And that, I suddenly understand, is what I'd like to pass on to another generation.

The passengers are filing off. I stand to the side. In a few minutes Michael appears. He is not in the same eager high spirits as when he left. He carries a knapsack and I can read the distress on his face.

He sees me immediately. I walk toward him and he barely knows what to say past hello.

He puts down the knapsack and we stand there.

"Bad news in Texas, huh?" I finally ask.

"Yeah, Bill," he answers sullenly. "I dunno. Sometimes the things you want most in life . . . They just don't work out."

"You have to face that and accept it, Mike," I tell him. "That's life. That's part of becoming a man."

Mike is looking at the knapsack. "I'd waited so long to meet my mom," he says. "All my life. You know how much I talked about it, Bill."

I nod, placing a hand on his shoulder.

"But after a day or two I could barely talk to her. Why couldn't I just hold her and call her Mom? That's all I wanted. I just wanted her to be my mother. Why couldn't that happen? Why can't I have a mother who loves me? Everybody else does."

"Mike, listen to me," I say. He looks up. "I don't have all the answers, either, but I can tell you this. Life isn't always fair and you can't expect it to be. But you know all about Texas now. You know about your mother, your grandmother, and your brothers. You know about your father from before. It's time to look in the other direction. You have to look at the future, not the past. If you do that, everything will fall into place. I promise you."

He doesn't seem convinced.

"Aw, Bill," he says. "You don't under——"

I start to grin. "I don't?"

He thinks about it. "I guess you do understand," he says, mustering his best teasing tone. "Some."

I pick up his knapsack. "Come on," I say to him. "Ma's got dinner ready and there's some fresh sheets on your bed. You won't recognize the house. We had the front porch fixed."

"What'd you do that for?"

"The house needed it."

"I liked the porch the way it was," he says.

"Too late," I tell him. "You weren't here to say anything."

"The second I leave," he protests, "everything gets out of control."

I take a playful swing at his arm. "Get moving!" I order, and he is through the exit doors ahead of me. We go to the parking lot and find my car. Moments later, we are on our way back to Staten Island, catching up on the time spent apart since April.

Michael has remained in our family since. That is not to say every moment has been easy. Life isn't like that. But in the months that have passed, I've been given cause for great optimism. With the important things, I think we are succeeding.

252

Home is, after all, where you are welcome and where you are loved. And where you choose to stay.

Staten Island, New York
May 1983